you can RENEW this item from
home by visiting our Website at
www.woodbridge.lioninc.org or by
calling (203) 389-3433

BIG BOB GIBSON'S BBQ BOOK

BIG BOB GIBSON'S
BBQ BOOK

RECIPES AND SECRETS FROM A
LEGENDARY BARBECUE JOINT

CHRIS LILLY

Clarkson Potter/Publishers
New York

Published in the United States by Clarkson Potter/Publishers, an imprint of
the Crown Publishing Group, a division of Random House, Inc., New York.
www.crownpublishing.com
www.clarksonpotter.com

CLARKSON POTTER is a trademark and POTTER with colophon is a
registered trademark of Random House, Inc.

Library of Congress Cataloging-in-Publication Data
Lilly, Chris.
Big Bob Gibson's BBQ book / Chris Lilly.
p.   cm.
1. Barbecue cookery.   2. Big Bob Gibson's BBQ (Firm).   I. Title.
TX840.B3L54   2009
641.7'6—dc22   2008050633

ISBN 978-0-307-40811-2

Printed in the United States of America

Design by Subtitle

10 9 8 7 6 5 4 3 2 1

First Edition

★　★　★　★　★

To my mother and father, for all the gifts they have
provided me through their example of how to live

To my wife, Amy, and children, Jacob, Andrew, and Caroline;
my life is the fullest when I am spending time with you

Big Bob Gibson, in 1956, proudly shows off his unique catering style.

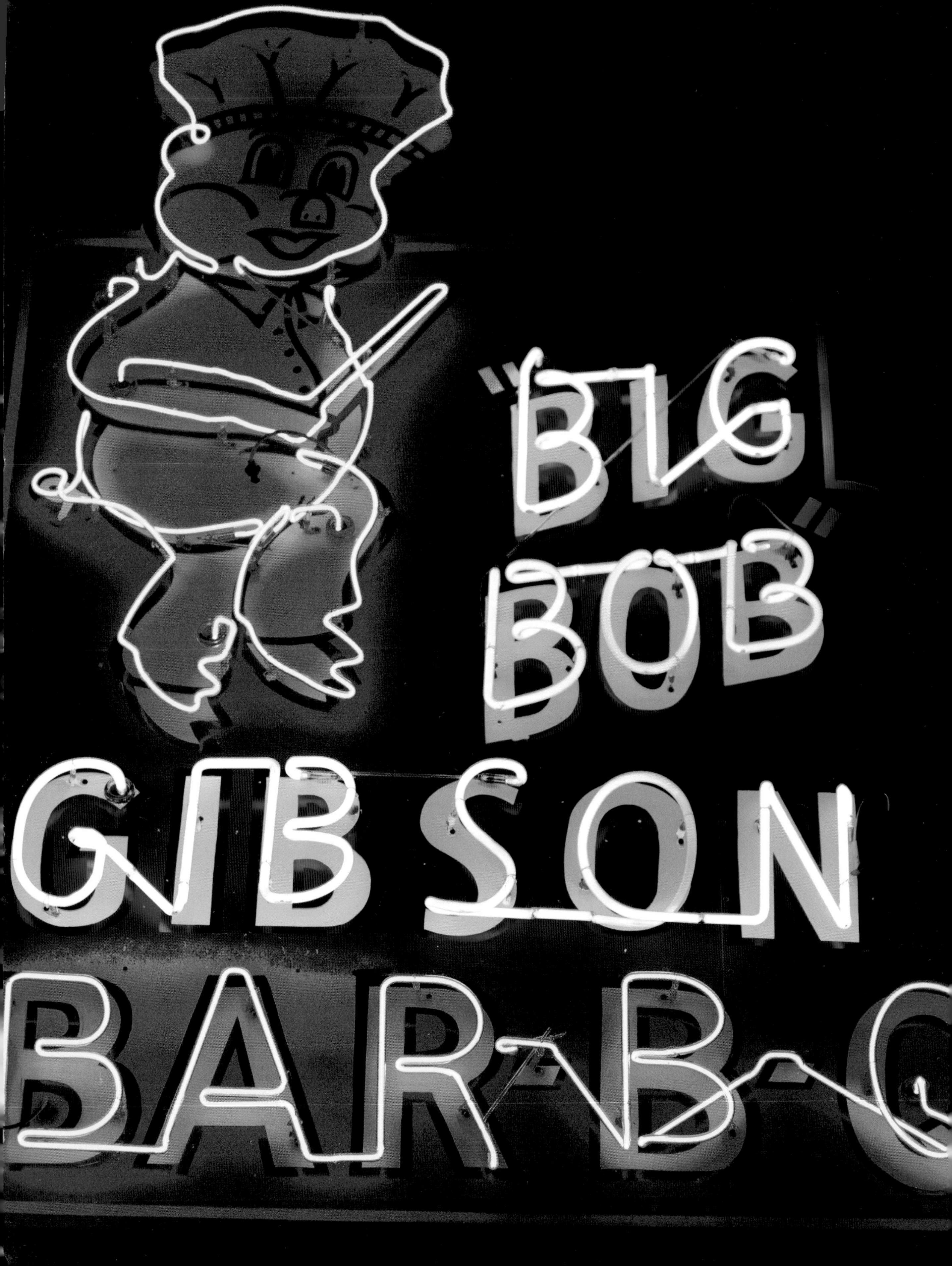
"BIG"
BOB
GIBSON
BAR-B-Q

CONTENTS

PREFACE

I began my new day, new job, new life blinded as a dense cloud of smoke engulfed my vision. This was not exactly what I had pictured when I stepped up to the podium to receive my college diploma, or when I was shopping for a new suit prior to my first interview. I really didn't know what to expect when I was hired at a restaurant with the history and tradition of Big Bob Gibson Bar-B-Q. My only instruction: "Dress casual." So there I stood in my khakis and polo shirt, waiting for a flood of tears to soothe my stinging eyes.

As my vision cleared, I felt as if I had traveled back in time fifty years and stepped into a black-and-white photograph in which light and shadows outlined gigantic brick ovens. The three enormous cookers were capped with a series of solid steel lids, each hinged and connected to the ceiling by a cable and pulley. The floor, walls, and ceiling were black and gray from years of smoke saturation. Fluorescent lights hidden behind stained yellow lenses did little to brighten the room. It was the shafts of sunshine flickering through the wall fan that lit the smokehouse and announced to everyone who entered that this was hallowed ground.

I staggered, disoriented and still half-blind, in the process brushing up against a silent figure who until then had remained unnoticed. It was evident he belonged there perched on an ancient hickory stump, its bark long ago worn away to leave a stool of smoked tanned hardwood indistinguishable from the old man's arms. His dull gray hair blended with the walls as perfectly as did his stained and tattered overalls. Only his smile stood out in the murky gray setting, and he gave me less a greeting and more a chuckle of bemusement as he waited to see what I would do next.

To break the awkward silence I announced, "Sir, I'm the new guy here to learn how to barbecue."

I soon realized he knew who I was and was aware that he was to teach me his trade. While his smile remained accepting, his eyes surveyed me frankly, trying to ascertain what he had to work with. Even without a word of conversation I felt he was able to assess my desire and potential unerringly, for I was in his world.

He rose, and the intimidation I had felt earlier grew exponentially as he towered over me. He was a big man, both tall and broad, but he stood with the youthful fluidness of someone half his age. He placed his hand on my shoulder reassuringly and said, "Take my seat, pay close attention, and open your mind. At the end of the day you'll tell me what you've learned." With that he left the pit-room, his baffling words lingering as I stood staring at the open door, waiting for more instruction or a hint that this was a joke played on all those new to cooking barbecue. Eventually I decided simply to play along, and I took the seat my mentor had proffered.

The stump was unexpectedly comfortable. Years of wear had hollowed a depression at the crest of the seat, making the block of wood feel like an executive's chair. As I pulled a notepad from my pocket to begin recording the day's lessons, I became aware of a beautiful aroma that made my stomach shift and my mouth water. Every drop of moisture in the air was tinged with the hypnotic aroma of Grandma's kitchen and a campfire grill rolled into one. The effect of this unexpected and pleasurable sensation was instant calm, and my anxieties melted away.

BBQ TIMELINE

5:00 a.m.	**BASTE PORK SHOULDERS ON PIT #1** **ADD 3 LOGS AND SPREAD COALS**
5:45 a.m.	**REMOVE BEEF FROM PIT #2**
6:15 a.m.	**REMOVE PORK SHOULDERS FROM PIT #1**
6:30 a.m.	**SEASON RIBS AND LOAD PIT #1** **ADD 2 LOGS AND SPREAD COALS**
7:00 a.m.	**SEASON CHICKENS AND LOAD PIT #3** **ADD 5 LOGS AND SPREAD COALS**
7:30 a.m.	**SEASON BEEF AND LOAD PIT #2** **ADD 4 LOGS AND SPREAD COALS**
8:00 a.m.	**DESERT PITROOM AND LEAVE ROOKIE Q'ER SITTING ON A STUMP**
8:45 a.m.	**FLIP RIBS ON PIT #1** **ADD 2 LOGS AND SPREAD COALS**
9:00 a.m.	**BASTE AND FLIP CHICKENS, SEASON WITH BLACK PEPPER** **ADD 3 LOGS AND SPREAD COALS**
9:45 a.m.	**IGNORE THE "GREENHORN" IN THE CORNER AND LEAVE THE ROOM**
10:30 a.m.	**REMOVE CHICKENS FROM PIT #3**
11:00 a.m.	**REMOVE RIBS FROM PIT #1**
11:30 a.m.	**SEASON RIBS AND LOAD PIT #1** **ADD 2 LOGS AND SPREAD COALS**
1:30 p.m.	**SEASON CHICKENS AND LOAD PIT #3** **ADD 5 LOGS AND SPREAD COALS**
3:15 p.m.	**FLIP RIBS ON PIT #1** **ADD 2 LOGS AND SPREAD COALS**
3:30 p.m.	**BASTE AND FLIP CHICKENS, SEASON WITH BLACK PEPPER** **ADD 3 LOGS AND SPREAD COALS**
4:00 p.m.	**REMOVE RIBS FROM PIT #1**
4:30 p.m.	**SEASON PORK SHOULDERS AND LOAD PIT #1** **ADD 5 LOGS AND SPREAD COALS**
4:45 p.m.	**REMOVE BEEF FROM PIT #2**
5:00 p.m.	**REMOVE CHICKENS FROM PIT #3**

Big Bob Gibson's eldest son, Floyd, stands proudly in front of the restaurant in the late 1920s.

As the day wore on, I began to pick up on the details of the pitroom process. There were flurries of activity centered on seasoning meat, flipping chickens, and tending the fire; but for the most part the job was defined by patient waiting. Where was the continuous basting and checking of doneness? The mad shuffle of food and employees that characterized the busy kitchens I'd known before was not evident. Every few hours the ovens opened to reveal a massive amount of meat on the cinder-block cookers. Forty whole pork shoulders were removed to make room for fifty slabs of ribs. Four hours passed as chickens in a pit were seasoned, smoked, flipped, and dipped into a vat of white barbecue sauce. The only thing that changed during this slow and steady rotation of barbecue was the aroma given off by each meat.

The hickory stool provided the perfect angle from which to observe everything in the room, and I noted each action. I imagined that a poster on the wall reflecting my "BBQ Timeline" would be a great help to everyone who worked the pits.

When the shafts of sunlight filtering through the wall fan lengthened and diffused, I knew my first day had come to an end. As the pitmaster entered the room one last time, I bounded from my stump, excited to report my day's findings, sure my diligent scribblings would impress anyone who viewed them. With the proud smile of a child showing off his first drawing, I handed him my log. I waved my arms exuberantly as I recited from memory what needed to be done and when, then stood, arms crossed, waiting for the praise that was sure to follow. I imagined he would appoint me to cook the following day because I so clearly knew how it was done.

With another all-knowing grin, he turned and spread a bed of coals before adding five more logs to carry the heat through the night. Inside the firebox, the flames glowed bright as my notebook was reduced to ash.

"You don't need a laundry list telling you what to do," he said. "Just sit on the stump and listen. The chickens will whisper to you when they need to be flipped. The pork will sing when it is finished cooking. The fire will wink at you when another log is needed. No list, no clock, no thermometer can tell you how to cook barbecue. You sit in the corner and you just know."

More than fifteen years later I'm still sitting on that stump listening to the pit.

"WITH ANOTHER ALL-KNOWING GRIN, HE TURNED AND SPREAD A BED OF COALS BEFORE ADDING FIVE MORE LOGS TO CARRY THE HEAT THROUGH THE NIGHT. INSIDE THE FIREBOX, THE FLAMES GLOWED BRIGHT AS MY NOTEBOOK WAS REDUCED TO ASH."

INTRODUCTION

A few years back I attended a food symposium and a speaker was asked the difference between barbecuing and grilling. He gave the textbook reply: "The process of barbecuing requires cooking at low temperatures for a long period of time, and the inverse describes grilling." While this is not technically incorrect, the word "barbecue" encompasses much more than smoker temperature and cooking time. Barbecue is also the time culture that surrounds the process and, more important, the memories that are created. It is the new friendships that are born and perpetuated while the meat simmers slowly in the outdoor cooker. Barbecue is the effect that the smoke and tempting smells have on people, acknowledged by smiles that are permanently imprinted on the minds of those that experience them. Stained clothes, sauce dripping from the chin of small children, and bones drying on the otherwise empty plates are the only outward sign that something glorious has been created, but feelings of accomplishment and fulfillment linger within the cook.

Learning to barbecue is a process, and no book, including this one, will confer this knowledge instantly. No written recipe, no matter how lengthy and detailed, can explain how to master a beef brisket. Not even a face-to-face crash course with the most astute pitmaster will transform you into a sultan of 'Q. Oh, I realize the dedication that some people devote to learning new things and conquering unknowns, but learning is the same as cooking barbecue. It takes time. Achieving the best results is a slow and time-consuming process. The art is only mastered through time and dedication. The good news is that the lessons along the way are almost as delicious and rewarding as reaching the ultimate goal of barbecue mastery.

Many barbecue beginners make the mistake of over-seasoning their barbecue with a combination of brines, marinades, rubs, and sauces, applying everything they have ever heard about cooking barbecue all at once. The result is generally a culinary catastrophe. Flavor is important, but the true measure of barbecue is the tenderness and moistness of the meat. The pinnacle of "low and slow" cannot be reached without knowing how to achieve that.

So how do you know when you can be labeled a "pitmaster"? The same way you'll come to recognize when your ribs are done: You just know! Imagine being able to produce consistently superior results every time you light your cooker. Now, with the same confidence, imagine doing it blindfolded. Your dry rub is perfectly blended, the cooker is maintaining your desired temperature, the brisket is not overdone, and your pork explodes with flavor. This level of mastery comes from repetition, trial and error, and perseverance. Congratulations if you make it to that level of oneness with your meat. Please don't quote me on that last line.

In most places mere mention of the word "barbecue" will result in a deep-seated controversy over not only the best kind but the very origin of the word. People from every country in the world feel their "low and slow" method of cooking is the best and lay claim to having invented the technique. It is not my intention to write an essay on the Spanish explorers, the Arawakan Indians, Taino "barbacoa," French "barbe a queue," or even Middle Eastern cookery. I choose to celebrate what we know today as barbecue and its American roots.

Two more generations of barbecuers: Big Bob's daughter, Punk, holding her son Don McLemore, in front of the old home place in 1942.

★ ★ ★ ★ ★

Barbecuing as we know it began to take hold with the migration of Europeans and Africans to the southern tier of North America. Cattle and pigs were transplanted to the New World and became the primary meat source for the colonists. The least desirable or largest cuts of meat were often reserved for the slaves, migrant workers, or lower-income people, who cooked them over a low fire to render the tough cuts more tender and palatable, producing succulent smoked results. Although the cooking method was labor intensive, the barbecued meat was inexpensive, and the cooking and eating of barbecue became the center of gatherings for friends and family.

My barbecue story begins in 1925. The home place of Robert Gibson, my wife Amy's great-grandfather, is located just outside of Decatur, Alabama. With a six-foot four-inch frame and weighing close to three hundred pounds, Bob Gibson had the stature and charismatic personality that made him a well-known figure in the area. His "never met a stranger" attitude endeared him to everyone he came across, and to one and all he was known as Big Bob.

Big Bob Gibson as he looked in 1925, the year he opened for business.

He was an uneducated but hardworking man who spent his days as an employee of the L&N Railroad (the Louisville and Nashville, that is). This manual labor kept him busy and though the income was steady, it was not nearly enough to support his family. Which, like everything else associated with Bob, was extremely large. His wife was Ellen Woodall Gibson, but as you can probably guess she had a nickname: Big Mama. Big Bob and Big Mama lived with their six children: Little Bob (Robert), Sister (Velma), Floyd, Cotton (David), Punk (Catherine), and Ruth (Sara Ruth).

With a small army of mouths to feed and a limited income, the home place gradually turned into a small farm. While Big Bob was away working for the railroad it was up to Big Mama, the kids, and a stiff-legged horse named Ole Dan to work the farm. A typical day included assigned chores for all the kids, and rest was sitting on the hitched farm equipment to supply extra weight while Ole Dan worked the land. The garden was ample, with a huge variety of vegetables. Adjacent to the garden was the barn, which gave entrance to the cow field and also flanked the pigpen. Chickens often wandered the yard when not penned up in the coop.

The busiest time of the year was the harvest, followed by the canning season. Big Mama's pantry was filled not with store-bought provisions but with Mason jars of vegetables, and there was nothing that she wouldn't can, including cooked sausage. Cucumbers were canned or pickled: To pickle them, Big Mama dropped the cukes into a wooden barrel filled with water, salt, and grape leaves, then set a circular slab of wood on top and weighted down the wood with a large rock to ensure that the soon-to-be-pickles remained completely submerged.

When needed, days were set aside for butchering hogs. It was not uncommon to find Big Bob and Big Mama side by side grinding homemade sausage and salting hams to cure in their smokehouse. The lives of the whole Gibson clan centered on food.

For all the labor involved in running a small farm during the week, it was the weekend that turned into something extra special for the family. If Big Bob wasn't working, he was cooking, and barbecue was his specialty. From his hand-dug pit, the aroma of hickory-smoked pork drifted lazily over the farms and fields of North Alabama, drawing people from miles away. At first the crowds consisted of friends and family, but soon acquaintances and strangers were showing up as well. One thing was for sure: When Big Bob was cooking 'Q, people gathered around the makeshift oak-plank table in his backyard hoping for a sample. The long lines and wide smiles made it clear to this L&N railroad worker that his future lay in barbecue.

One of Big Bob's first obstacles in moving from backyard sales to an actual restaurant specializing in authentic slow-cooked barbecue was the cooker itself. Big Bob's smoker consisted of a hand-dug pit, a couple of wire racks, and two sheets of tin. Duplicating that smoker in the restaurant was both impractical and unsanitary, yet he was adamant that if he was going to sell barbecue from a storefront, he would not compromise on the quality by offering anything less than real "pit barbecue."

His solution was to raise his pit above ground by building a large brick coffin with bricks forming double walls around two large raised grates. The brick box was covered with large sheets of corrugated metal. There were open slots every two feet at the bottom of the brick walls, so hot coals could be shoveled into the cooker. A huge brick chimney at the end of the pit transferred the smoke from the outdoor pavilion.

One element Big Bob refused to compromise on was the pit floor, insisting it be red clay, just as it was in his backyard. The clay floor provided a base for the hot coals and absorbed the grease from the meat. Every week the spent coals, ash, and top layer of dirt were shoveled from the cooker floor to a depth of two feet and replaced with fresh red clay. Waiting any longer to shovel the grease-saturated floor would be a fire hazard, a phenomenon Big Bob experienced firsthand on several occasions.

"THE SPEED AT WHICH YOU BECOME A PITMASTER IS DIRECTLY PROPORTIONAL TO THE SIZE OF YOUR TEACHER'S ASH PILE."

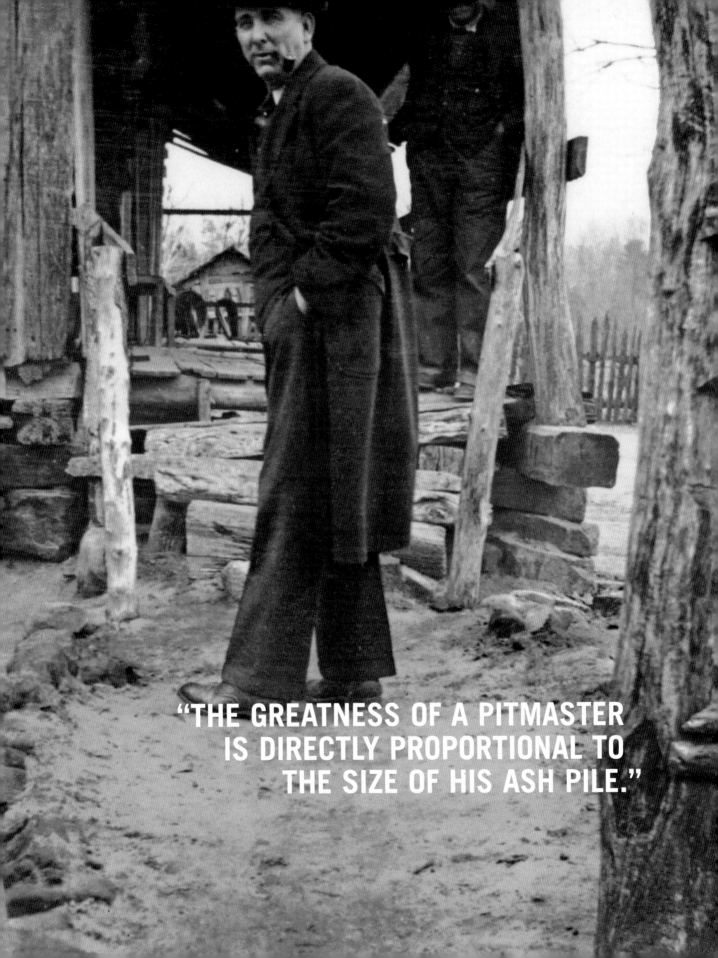

"THE GREATNESS OF A PITMASTER IS DIRECTLY PROPORTIONAL TO THE SIZE OF HIS ASH PILE."

CHAPTER 1

GET-TING TING READY

★ ★ ★ ★ ★

BIG BOB MADE SOME IMPORTANT DECISIONS PRIOR TO

welcoming his first customer in 1925. He built a freestanding pit to cook in, he chose hickory as his fuel source, and he selected a combination of seasonings to use on the meat. For an uneducated man, transferring business from the backyard to a storefront was a major task. This was an undertaking Big Bob couldn't possibly do by himself. He needed someone who was experienced with barbecue who could share in the decision making, the workload, and the initial investment. He turned to Big Mama's brother, Sam Woodall.

From these humble beginnings grew a legacy that would affect both the Gibson and the Woodall families for future generations. This style of barbecue would define the flavors of this region in years to come and establish northern Alabama as a barbecue hotbed. Now Big Bob Gibson Bar-B-Q is a destination; people travel there to enjoy Big Bob's legacy by sampling the simple honest flavors of his barbecue.

Exploring Big Bob's choices back in 1925 will help the present-day barbecuer make some of the same important decisions on the road to defining his or her own barbecue style. Since Bob Gibson or Sam Woodall can't walk you through this process and act as a batter-board for ideas, this chapter will do the same.

★ ★ ★ ★ ★

COOKER SETUP

Today the avid barbecue chef must overcome very different obstacles. Big Bob cooked his 'Q in a pit. Most barbecue today is made in backyard cookers with either direct-fired gas or charcoal grills. One problem that surfaces is how to cook "low and slow" on grills set up to cook "hot and fast." Another hurdle is getting maximum efficiency from the grill's firebox.

There is no exact difference in cooking temperature between barbecuing and grilling. Many cooking procedures will include both styles: for example, cooking ribs over indirect heat at a low temperature and then caramelizing a sweet finishing glaze over direct heat. For that reason it is advantageous to set up two zones on a grill. The first zone is used for grilling or searing foods. The second zone provides indirect heat, allowing foods to cook slowly.

The next few pages contain information, tips, and diagrams covering barbecue attack strategies. But we're not dealing with an enemy; we are working to complete a goal of barbecue perfection. The same military strategies used to conquer a battlefield can be used to master the backyard cooker: The Indirect Strategy, Encirclement Strategy, Bypass Strategy, and Flank Strategy guarantee success with indirect cooking.

SINGLE COOKING CHAMBER GRILL— INDIRECT STRATEGY

When direct grilling will not yield moist and tender results it is imperative that a backyard chef move to an indirect barbecue strategy. This type of strategy consists of cooking away from direct flame. There is no ideal indirect cooking method for every backyard grill. The cooker used will dictate which indirect strategy should be used.

The easiest way to cook low and slow on a backyard grill is to build a charcoal fire on one side of the cooking chamber and place your meat on the other side. A water pan may be added during the cooking process to add moisture to the cooking chamber and keep the meat from drying out.

The biggest problem with this method is the need to add charcoal every hour to maintain a low and steady temperature over a long cooking period. This cooker setup requires a diligent monitoring of the thermometer for an extended period.

GAS GRILL—INDIRECT STRATEGY

Most modern gas grills have two, three, or four burners; use this to your advantage when barbecuing. Just because you have multiple burners doesn't mean you need to light them all. Start by lighting only one side burner and keep it on low. Place the meat to be cooked away from the hot burner.

When using this strategy, remember that even though you are cooking away from the fire, the food closest to the heat will get done the quickest. When using this method, rotating your food is a must to ensure an even doneness throughout your 'Q.

Opposite: Adding liquid creates moist heat within a closed grill.
Overleaf left and right: The indirect strategy creates a cooking zone away from the coals. Place larger cuts of meat such as lamb shanks away from the coals on a closed grill for even cooking.

★ PITMASTER'S TIP ★

When cooking for a long period, always keep a lit charcoal chimney on standby to add hot coals to your cooker as needed. Placing unlit charcoal on top of lit coals will temporarily smother your fire and cause the temperature in your cooker to drop until the fire catches up.

CYLINDER COOKER— INDIRECT STRATEGY

This cylinder or bullet-type grill is a great cooker on which to learn barbecue basics, and it is the cooker of choice for many barbecue veterans. Even though the firebox is directly beneath the cooking grate, the drip pan acts as a deflector shield for the intense heat. One advantage of this type of unit is that access to the firebox can be gained through a side door, so it's easy to check on your fire or refuel it without opening the lid and losing valuable heat and moisture.

To gain maximum cook time without having to refuel, a creative version of the Minion Method is the preferred lighting procedure. The Minion Method, popularized by Jim Minion, extends the life of your fire by adding both lit and unlit charcoal to the firebox. Cut the bottom out of a coffee can and place the can in the center of the fire grate. Surround the can completely with unlit charcoal. Sprinkle wood chips over the unlit charcoal. Fill the can with white-hot charcoal, then immediately lift out the can.

Crack the dampers to allow a minimal amount of air to the fire. The charcoal will slowly burn from the center to the outer edges. This simple procedure will add hours to your cook time and free up valuable time to focus on other barbecue necessities.

KETTLE GRILL— ENCIRCLEMENT STRATEGY

When cooking for long periods of time on a kettle grill the encirclement strategy is a great option. This method works by placing a ring of charcoal around the meat and allowing the fire just enough oxygen that it barely burns around the ring. It provides a stable cooking temperature for as long as six hours. Another advantage to this method is that it cooks all sides of the food evenly, which makes turning meat unnecessary.

To execute the encirclement strategy, place a stainless-steel bowl, with a twelve-inch diameter, in the center of the kettle. Fill the bowl halfway with water or a mixture of water, fruit juice, and seasoning for added flavor. Create a C-shaped ring of charcoal around the bowl, leaving an eight-inch open gap on one side. Fill the gap with white hot charcoal, close the lid, and begin the cooking process. Keep the grill dampers wide open until the desired cooking temperature is reached, then close all the dampers to approximately one quarter inch per opening.

Opposite: Cook all day on an upright cylinder cooker; use a coffee can to arrange the hot coals.

⋆ PITMASTER'S TIP ⋆

Drip pans are a great tool to prevent the fat rendered from your barbecue from dripping onto hot coals and causing flare-ups. The pans can also provide a buffer between a firebox and cooking grate, turning a direct cooker into an indirect cooker. Take advantage of this pan by filling it halfway with a mixture of water, fruit juice, and seasonings to fill your cooker with flavored moisture. Don't use pure fruit juice because the sugars in juice can scorch and negatively affect the flavor of your meat; instead a fifty-fifty ratio of water and juice works great.

BARREL GRILL— BYPASS STRATEGY

This is a strategy that can gain you valuable cook time when cooking in a single-chamber grill. A line of charcoal slowly burns from one side of the cooker to the other, thus bypassing your barbecue. This is another method that works by only allowing enough oxygen to the fire so it barely burns across the cooker, providing an extended cook time. When a long-term cook is needed, the bypass strategy is your best bet when using a single-chamber grill.

To create a bypass setup, arrange unlit charcoal in a line across the bottom of a barrel-style grill. Light one end of the charcoal and close the lid, leaving all the grill dampers wide open. When the desired cooking temperature is reached, close all of the dampers almost completely. Most cookers of this type are not airtight at the seams, so the fire will draw plenty of air through the cracks. To begin cooking, place your barbecue away from the fire. Over the next several hours your fire will creep toward the items cooking on the grill. A quick shift of your 'Q from one side of the grill to the other will ensure even, indirect cooking heat through the entire process.

BARREL GRILL— FLANK STRATEGY

This simple strategy provides even, indirect heat throughout your grill. The flank strategy is ideal for short to medium indirect cooks. The advantage is that there is no need to rotate your food, because even heat is created on each side of your 'Q. I wouldn't advise using this method for a long cook because refueling two charcoal piles would be very inconvenient.

To try the flank strategy, place a small pile of charcoal at each end of the barrel. Light each pile and open the bottom dampers at each end of the cooker. When the desired temperature is reached, close all of the dampers to approximately one quarter inch. As soon as the cooker temperature levels out, place the food in the middle of the cooking grate between the piles of charcoal. Regulate the temperature of the grill during the cooking process by adjusting the dampers; open for a hotter fire and closed for a cooler burn.

⋆ PITMASTER'S TIP ⋆

Many grills come with a temperature gauge that reads: Smoke, Barbecue, and Grill. Remove this immediately and throw it as far as you can. Instead, get a thermometer with actual numerical temperature readings, and install it near the cooking grate for the most accurate reading.

WOOD SELECTION

With Big Bob's restaurant opening imminent and the building and cooker in place, he still had to choose what kind of wood to use. This is a decision that often leaves the most astute pitmaster scratching his head. Big Bob used mostly hickory and oak wood, which was cut from trees cleared from the old home place. Based on trial and error and advice from trusted friends who were veteran backyard barbecue tasters, Big Bob decided that hickory was his best choice, for three reasons. First, hickory was very plentiful in North Alabama. With only one barbecue stand in the county, he figured he would have an infinite supply. Second, the price was right. During the 1920s oak, though also abundant in Alabama, was considered a more desirable wood than hickory for furniture and lumber. Third, and most important, smoldering hickory wood gave his meat a depth of smoke flavor unmatched by other woods.

Of course, all hickory is not created equal. In fact there are twelve species of hickory in the United States:

SCRUB HICKORY *Carya floridana*

PIGNUT HICKORY *Carya glabra*

NUTMEG HICKORY *Carya myristiciformis*

RED HICKORY *Carya ovalis*

SHAGBARK HICKORY *Carya ovata*

SHELLBARK HICKORY *Carya laciniosa*

SAND HICKORY *Carya pallida*

BLACK HICKORY *Carya texana*

MOCKERNUT HICKORY *Carya tomentosa*

WATER HICKORY *Carya aquatica*

BITTERNUT HICKORY *Carya cordiformis*

PECAN *Carya illinoiensis*

Of these twelve species, only five are stacked in the wood racks behind Big Bob Gibson Bar-B-Q today: Pignut, Red, Shagbark, Bitternut, and Pecan. These types of hickory are most common in our region. Over the years we have determined that each type of hickory carries a slightly different flavor profile. In log-to-log taste tests conducted over the course of eight decades, the winning hickory is the Pignut, because it carries a very deep smoke flavor with a less aggressive pungency.

The variety of woods that can be used for barbecuing is almost endless. Keep in mind that different woods will not only alter the flavor profile of your meats but will change the potency of dry rub and sauce as well. If you cook two slabs of ribs with the same dry rub but cook one over cherry wood and one over hickory, different spices within your dry rub will come to the forefront. Cherry tends to highlight the sweeter spices (such as cinnamon), while hickory will dull the sharper spices and bring out the earthy flavors (such as cumin or coriander). Sometimes it takes a mixture of woods to bring a dry rub or sauce to its full flavor potential.

Most avid barbecuers select a wood that is native to their region and learn to master the flavor it imparts. The wood type should be the one constant during your 'Q trials. Many people make the mistake of changing too many variables when cooking barbecue and end up with a culinary mess. Only after many backyard successes should you integrate new wood types into your regimen.

Not only is the variety of wood critical, its age is an important factor to consider as well. The desired taste of the food should be the most important consideration in determining how long to age your wood. Fresh-cut wood is referred to as "green," and the greener the wood, the stronger and often more bitter the smoke's flavor. Dry wood burns fast and has less flavor. After three months cut wood can be referred to as seasoned or aged. The longer wood sits after cutting, the dryer it gets. When burned, seasoned wood will emit a less pungent aroma.

Opposite: The pitmaster's day begins and ends the same way—with a wheelbarrow full of wood.

A fresh-cut pile of "green" hickory is stacked in front of wood ready for the pit.

Big Bob Gibson learned quickly how important it was to rotate his wood pile at the restaurant. He found that freshly cut or "green" wood smolders longer than aged or "seasoned" wood, which burns hotter and quicker. When cooking overnight it is important to use woods that have been aged similarly in order to control the cook time and fire temperature. Early on Big Bob decided it was best to use the FIFO method (first-in first-out) with his woodpile, although he had a different name for it. As Big Bob explained to his employees, he called it the RTDW method, for "rotate the damn wood." This ensured he was always using wood that had been seasoned for approximately four months.

"WANNA KNOW HOW GOOD A BARBECUE RESTAURANT IS? TAKE A LOOK AT THE SIZE OF THEIR WOODPILE."
BIG BOB GIBSON

★ PITMASTER'S TIP ★

Newcomers to barbecue should not start with an all-wood fire; instead use a combination of charcoal and wood. Many make the mistake of over-smoking their meat using all wood, giving the resulting barbecue an acrid taste. This bitterness can give beginners a bad taste for bad 'Q! Think of wood as a seasoning rather than a fuel source. The more experience you have, the more wood you can use.

WOOD TYPE	FLAVOR	RECOMMENDED FOODS
ALDER	DELICATE WOOD-SMOKED FLAVOR	FISH AND SEAFOOD, INCLUDING TROUT, SWORDFISH, AND SALMON
APPLE	DENSE FRUITY FLAVOR, SLIGHTLY SWEET SMOKE	PORK, ESPECIALLY HAM; POULTRY; GAME BIRDS
APRICOT	MILDLY PUNGENT, SLIGHTLY SWEET SMOKE	PORK, CHICKEN
CHERRY	MILD FRUIT FLAVOR, SLIGHTLY SWEET SMOKE	PORK, POULTRY, GAME BIRDS
HICKORY	STRONG SMOKE FLAVOR, SLIGHTLY PUNGENT	PORK, BEEF, POULTRY, WILD GAME
MAPLE	MILD-SWEET SMOKY FLAVOR	PORK, POULTRY, VEGETABLES, GAME BIRDS
MESQUITE	STRONG PUNGENT EARTHY FLAVOR	BEEF, STEAKS, VEGETABLES
PEACH	MILDLY SWEET, WOODSY SMOKE	PORK, CHICKEN
PECAN	MEDIUM STRONG, SLIGHTLY PUNGENT/BITTER	TURKEY, CHICKEN, BEEF, PORK, WILD GAME
PIMENTO	SPICY PUNGENT SMOKE, SLIGHTLY PEPPERY	PORK, CHICKEN
OAK	MEDIUM-HEAVY SMOKE	BEEF, POULTRY

Opposite: A dry rub seasoning is one of the most important elements in creating a pile of sumptuous ribs.

SEASONING

Big Bob Gibson Bar-B-Q only had two main-course items on the menu when the doors first opened for customers. In the North Alabama region pork and chicken were the meat items that were most readily available for the new barbecue restaurant. As far as Big Bob was concerned, these two meat selections fully encompassed "barbecue," except of course for the occasional goat. A wide variety of side items (coleslaw, Golden Flake potato chips, and Brunswick stew) rounded out the Big Bob Gibson Bar-B-Q menu. Having such limited offerings made it easy to list the eat-in menu on a chalkboard. Big Bob was also proud to offer to-go menus, which he printed in his illegible scrawl on the back of a paper napkin.

When Big Bob started selling barbecue and side items in 1925 his spice rack was extensive, and largely empty. Salt, black pepper, and red pepper were his seasonings of choice. Beyond those there was only the dust and ash that settled on the empty spice shelf. Although we use a much more diverse range of seasonings today, especially in our competition recipes, I believe it is entirely possible to make extraordinary barbecue using just those basic seasonings. For his pork shoulders, salt was the seasoning Big Bob chose. He applied a thick coat of salt (one third cup) to the outside of the entire shoulder prior to placing it on the pit. Salt and black pepper were used on all of Big Bob's barbecue chickens. He stayed true to his "keep it simple" approach.

Whether chicken and pork were the only two meats to ever make it into Big Bob's Brunswick stew pot is unclear. He was, after all, an avid hunter, and both squirrel and rabbit are plentiful in Alabama. What we do know is that he emptied the spice rack when he made up a batch of stew in his twenty-gallon pots, adding not only salt and black pepper but red pepper, too. The spice rack didn't receive a new addition until the late 1940s, when beef was added to the menu and granulated garlic was introduced. Big Bob always knew you can produce great barbecue with only basic spices, as most of the secrets of barbecue reside in the cooking process itself. Nonetheless, most meats will benefit from a judicious seasoning, as it adds yet another layer of flavor.

Today, Big Bob Gibson Bar-B-Q has enlarged on that meager selection of spices, using four different dry rubs to season our meat. It is very difficult to alter any aspect of a business that has thrived since 1925, but no business can survive without change, and many changes there have been since Big Bob Gibson opened his doors more than eighty years ago. However, these changes were not instituted without careful review. Guidelines were set up to ensure any changes in recipes, ingredients, or cooking techniques were thoroughly tested and deemed exceptional before we introduced them to the public. First, all changes had to be accepted by 90 percent of the staff and management. Second and most important, any alterations had to be approved by a test group of customers who have frequented Big Bob's for more than thirty years. While new customers might have different ideas of what barbecue should taste like, we wanted to please the old-timers who grew up knowing and loving Big Bob Gibson Bar-B-Q. If those qualifications weren't demanding enough, any new recipe must be a World Barbecue Championship winner. All four dry rubs met and exceeded these guidelines, and I think you'll agree they carry on the Big Bob Gibson tradition of serving exceptional barbecue.

When mixing a dry rub it is important to approach your formula methodically. It is easy to open up a spice cabinet and do the "pinch of this, pinch of that" thing, but the results are often not good, and they're impossible to re-create if they are good! We use the following process in the restaurant to produce outstanding dry rubs. Following these guidelines will enable you to create your own signature spice blend.

MAKING A DRY RUB

First, break your dry seasonings down into four groups: Salts and Sugars, Pepper, Transition Spices, and Signature Flavors. When I conduct "How to Make a Dry Rub" classes, I literally set up a station for each group, so the unique attributes and benefits of each can be appreciated individually as the dry rub is "built."

SALTS AND SUGARS

When mixing a dry rub for barbecue, the first thing to consider is the ratio of sugar to salt. The type of food you are planning to cook and its cook time will play a big part in determining this ratio. For my taste, beef, fish, and wild game benefit from a rub with a high salt content and a smaller percentage of sugar. On the other hand, pork accepts a dry rub with more sugar than salt extremely well. In general, the longer the cooking time, the less sugar should be added in order to prevent premature sugar caramelization, which can yield burnt barbecue or a blackened appearance.

Taste each of the salts and sugars available to you (see the list below for some suggestions), then combine the varieties you like in a balance that suits your personal preference. If your diet dictates, it is completely acceptable to skip the salt or sugar or both altogether. Once you get the salt-to-sugar ratio where you want it, proceed to the pepper.

Salt
Refined, fine grained (included in Big Bob's secret Pork Shoulder Seasoning)

Kosher salt
Additive-free, coarse grained

Sea salt
From evaporated sea water; usually either coarse or very fine grained. Generally less pronounced saline flavor than table salt.

Seasoned salt
Regular salt combined with flavoring ingredients: garlic salt, onion salt, celery salt

Salt substitutes
An alternative for those who require a low sodium diet

White sugar
Common, highly refined cane or beet sugar. Will scorch at hotter temps

Brown sugar
White sugar combined with molasses. Adds color and flavor to barbecue

Turbinado sugar
Steam-cleaned raw sugar. Light molasses flavor. Great for extended cook times because the burn point is higher than that of other sugars

SAMPLE RUB: STEP 1

¼ CUP WHITE SUGAR
¼ CUP BROWN SUGAR
2 TABLESPOONS GARLIC SALT
2 TABLESPOONS KOSHER SALT

PEPPER

Successful dry rubs need to be well balanced not only in flavor but also in heat. Different peppers have different flavor and heat profiles. Cayenne pepper is slightly bitter and provides an instant hit of heat, while black pepper has a mid-spectrum heat with an earthy flavor, and white pepper provides background warmth with a light pepper flavor. These pepper types can be mixed to provide a balanced spice.

Add ground pepper to the salt-sugar mix in small increments until your ideal mix of heat and flavor is reached. Remember, adding more pepper is always an option, but you can't remove pepper from a seasoning mix, so go slow!

Cayenne pepper
Also called ground red pepper, a pungent powder made from a variety of dried chiles. A taste provides instant or front-end heat.

White pepper

Lighter in color and milder in flavor; provides a gentle heat and background warmth

Black pepper

The world's most popular spice; it's not the hottest but it has a stronger flavor than white or cayenne peppers. Fine or coarse ground, it works well in all barbecue applications.

Ground chile powder

Not to be confused with chili (chili with an "i") powder. Can be made from a wide variety of dried chiles. Flavors vary from very hot to mild. Smoked chile powders such as ground chipotle are also widely available.

SAMPLE RUB: STEP 2

¼ CUP WHITE SUGAR

¼ CUP BROWN SUGAR

2 TABLESPOONS GARLIC SALT

2 TABLESPOONS KOSHER SALT

1 TEASPOON CAYENNE PEPPER

1 TEASPOON BLACK PEPPER

TRANSITION SPICES

At this point you should have a dry rub that is well balanced but not well rounded. Keep in mind you are working on two different ends of the flavor spectrum. The salt-sugar ratio and pepper profile should be pleasing but could taste spiky and not united at this point. Transition spices unite these two elements to create a seamless flavor.

The following list highlights a few suggested transition spices. These can be added with a relatively heavy hand because their flavors are not as dominant as those of other spices. Notice also the color variations of the transition spices. A successful dry rub will not only supply a fantastic flavor to your barbecue but will also provide an appealing color to the "bark," or outside of barbecue, which is often the most flavorful area.

Chili powder

Seasoning mixture of dried chiles, garlic, cumin, coriander, oregano, and cloves; deep brownish-rust-red in color; pungent earthy flavor. Use with *beef, lamb, pork,* and *wild game.*

Cumin

Aromatic with a nutty, light peppery flavor; ground cumin varies in shades of brown. Use with *beef, poultry, fish, pork,* and *seafood.*

Paprika

Flavor ranges from mild to pungent and hot; color ranges from orange-red to bloodred. Hungarian paprika has a deeper, heartier flavor while Spanish paprika has a milder flavor; smoked paprika is also widely available. Use with *beef, poultry, fish, pork,* and *seafood.*

SAMPLE RUB: STEP 3

¼ CUP WHITE SUGAR

¼ CUP BROWN SUGAR

2 TABLESPOONS GARLIC SALT

2 TABLESPOONS KOSHER SALT

1 TEASPOON CAYENNE PEPPER

1 TEASPOON BLACK PEPPER

¼ CUP PAPRIKA

1 TEASPOON GROUND CUMIN

SIGNATURE FLAVORS

Congratulations! You have now created a basic barbecue dry rub. This combination of flavors represents most of what's contained in the successful barbecue seasonings on the market. This blend will give your barbecue a very good flavor as is, but if you take it a step further, you can customize your rub with truly individual flavor. Add your favorite spices and dry herbs in small increments to define your favorite flavors and stamp your name on all of your backyard offerings. The following is a short list of flavors and serving applications that we use when cooking barbecue at home and around the country.

Allspice
Ground pimento berry; tastes like a combination of cinnamon, nutmeg, and cloves. A signature of Jamaican jerk cooking. Use with *pork* and *chicken*.

Basil
Pungent, licorice/clove flavor. Use with *fish* and *poultry*.

Cardamom
Member of the ginger family with a warm, spicy-sweet flavor. Use with *pork (ham)*.

Celery seed
Warm, earthy celery smell and flavor. Use with *fish* and *poultry*.

Cinnamon
Mildly sweet to bittersweet flavor. Use with *pork* and *beef*.

Cloves
Pungent peppery flavor. Use with *pork (ham)* and *wild game*.

Coriander
An intense, sweet, aromatic flavor that tastes like a combination of lemon and sage. Use with *pork, lamb, poultry,* and *beef*.

Dill
Distinctive light, earthy flavor. Use with *chicken* and *fish*.

Fennel seed
Strong anise-like flavor that gets less intense when cooked. Use with *fish, pork, poultry,* and *beef*.

Garlic powder
A staple flavor for most barbecue items. Use with *pork, beef, lamb, poultry, seafood,* and *wild game*.

Ginger
Peppery and slightly sweet with a spicy aroma. Use with *wild game, fish, seafood, pork,* and *poultry*.

Mace
Slightly sweet and heavier pungent flavor than nutmeg. Use with *wild game, pork, poultry,* and *beef*.

Marjoram
Mild-bitter, sweet, oregano-like flavor. Use with *beef, poultry, lamb, fish, pork,* and *wild game*.

MSG
Or monosodium glutamate; no flavor but acts as an agent to intensify the flavor of savory foods. MSG causes allergic reactions in some people. Use with *beef, poultry, lamb, fish, pork, seafood,* and *wild game*.

Mustard powder
Strong pungent flavor, which heightens when moisture is added. Use with *beef, lamb, poultry, pork,* and *wild game*.

Nutmeg
Warm, slightly sweet and pungent flavor. Use with *pork* and *poultry*.

Onion powder
Versatile but pungent flavor and odor. Use with *pork, lamb, poultry, beef, seafood,* and *wild game*.

Oregano
Strong pungent spicy flavor and aroma. Use with *lamb, beef,* and *fish*.

Rosemary
Lemon/pine flavor and highly aromatic. Use with *fish* and *poultry*.

Sage
Slightly bitter with a musty mint flavor. Use with *lamb, pork,* and *poultry*.

Tarragon
Dominant anise-like or licorice flavor. Use with *fish, lamb, pork, poultry,* and *seafood*.

Thyme
Slightly pungent with a mint/lemon flavor and aroma. Use with *beef, fish, pork,* and *poultry*.

Turmeric
Brilliant yellow-orange color and bitter, pungent flavor. Use with *poultry*.

SAMPLE RUB: FINAL BLEND

¼ CUP WHITE SUGAR

¼ CUP BROWN SUGAR

2 TABLESPOONS GARLIC SALT

2 TABLESPOONS KOSHER SALT

1 TEASPOON CAYENNE PEPPER

1 TEASPOON BLACK PEPPER

¼ CUP PAPRIKA

1 TEASPOON GROUND CUMIN

¼ TEASPOON GROUND CORIANDER

⅛ TEASPOON ALLSPICE

Here are some other classic rub blends from my kitchen. Try these or experiment with your own creation.

SAMPLE RUB #2

8 TEASPOONS SEASONED SALT

4 TEASPOONS DARK BROWN SUGAR

1 TABLESPOON SUGAR

1 TABLESPOON PAPRIKA

½ TEASPOON BLACK PEPPER

½ TEASPOON GARLIC POWDER

¼ TEASPOON MUSTARD POWDER

¼ TEASPOON GROUND CUMIN

⅛ TEASPOON GROUND GINGER

SAMPLE RUB #3

¼ CUP DARK BROWN SUGAR

4 TEASPOONS GARLIC SALT

2 TEASPOONS SALT

½ TEASPOON CELERY SALT

4 TEASPOONS CHILI POWDER

1 TEASPOON BLACK PEPPER

¼ TEASPOON CAYENNE PEPPER

¼ TEASPOON WHITE PEPPER

¼ TEASPOON GROUND CINNAMON

SAMPLE RUB #4

4 TEASPOONS SALT

2½ TEASPOONS BLACK PEPPER

2 TEASPOONS PAPRIKA

2 TEASPOONS GARLIC POWDER

½ TEASPOON DRIED THYME

½ TEASPOON DRIED ROSEMARY

¼ TEASPOON CELERY SEED

★ PITMASTER'S TIP ★

Keep in mind, when working with dry-rub spices, that the full effect of the rub cannot be realized until it is tasted on cooked foods. Flavors can mellow or become stronger during the cooking process. Cinnamon, for example, might taste perfect in a dry-rub blend, but the flavor can amplify on your 'Q if covered with a sweet sauce.

CHAPTER 2

ODE
TO
PORK

★ ★ ★ ★ ★

WHICH CAME FIRST, THE PIG OR THE BARBECUE?

Fossils of wild pig-type animals indicate that there was a porcine
presence throughout Europe and Asia forty million years ago, so I
would say the pig wins that argument, hooves down. In 1539 Hernando
de Soto landed in what is now Tampa Bay, Florida, and introduced pigs
to North America. In three short years an initial cargo of thirteen pigs
had become a herd of seven hundred, despite numerous raids after
Native Americans developed a taste for pork.

As the number of colonists arriving in the New World grew, more
pigs were brought to America. As early as 1607, pigs were brought to
the Jamestown colony by Sir Walter Raleigh. With the population and
popularity of pigs growing, so too did the number of wild pigs in the
New York colonies. In fact, settlers on Manhattan Island ultimately
built a wall to control the roaming herds of pigs, causing the area to be
known then and today as Wall Street.

After the Revolutionary War, many pioneers began to head west with
pigs in tow. Large pig farms were soon popping up in Tennessee,
Kentucky, and Ohio, and along with them commercial slaughterhouses.
Cincinnati was the home of the first of many packing houses that
prospered in the major cities of the Midwest.

★ ★ ★ ★ ★

Throughout the nineteenth century, demand for pork made it necessary to move pigs to eastern markets. In 1826 alone, an estimated two hundred thousand pigs were moved out of Kentucky and Tennessee into North Carolina. Drovers were in charge of the task of herding these animals over long distances. Each drove consisted of about one hundred head, and the herd could only move five to eight miles per day depending on the lay of the land and how long the drovers had to search for stray pigs. Armed with a conch shell to call their herd and wagonloads of corn feed, drovers cleared wide swaths of land as they marched to market. These paths eventually developed into railroad routes. Who would have imagined that the pig was instrumental in the development of our railway system?

The history of pigs in this country makes it easy to understand the popularity of pork barbecue in the Southeast. In this barbecue hotbed, if you go to any restaurant and ask for a barbecue sandwich, you can expect pork. Your only choices are usually chopped or pulled. Although the origin of barbecue pork cooking techniques can be debated, the mastery of the art cannot; it's in the Southeast!

The two most important factors in successful pork cooking are the start and the finish. Unlike beef, pork does not need to go through an aging process to heighten flavor and increase tenderness, so choose fresh pork that is light red-pink in color with plenty of fat marbling. Another important element in a successful barbecue is learning to recognize when the barbecue is done. All of the best dry rubs, injections, and sauces in the world won't save your pork if you don't know when to take it off the grill.

Sometimes the simplest cooking method yields the best results. There is no better example than Big Bob Gibson's original recipe for pork shoulder. It is not the complex seasonings that made this pork stand out but his cooking procedure. For his original barbecue, only two ingredients are needed: a pork shoulder, and about one third cup of salt.

Here are his instructions; for those who need a few more clarifications and benchmarks along the way, see page 53.

Build a hickory wood fire in the brick pit away from the cooking grate. The metal lid above the firebox should be too hot to touch, but the doors above the cooking grate should be comfortably hot to your hand.

Cover the entire pork shoulder, including the skin, with an even coat of salt. Place the pork shoulder, skin side up, on the cooking grate.

As the hickory wood turns to coals, shovel the glowing embers directly underneath the shoulder. Add more wood to the fire as needed to replenish the supply of coals. Continue to shovel hot coals under the shoulders during the entire cooking process.

When the skin on the shoulder turns a deep golden brown, turn the pork over so the skin faces down. Wet the pork shoulder with the Big Bob Gibson Bar-B-Q Vinegar Sop Mop (see page 222). Continue cooking until the blade bone releases with a firm tug.

★　★　★　★　★

Since all cuts of pork are vastly different, there are a multitude of cooking methods and seasonings that produce the best results. Whether it is Big Bob's recipe for whole pork shoulder or instructions on how to cook butts, loin, bacon, ribs, or tenderloin, this chapter is packed with pork know-how.

Below: Big Bob Gibson, the barbecue entrepreneur, poses beside the restaurant in the 1930s with Mr. Dearman, a friend of the family.
Overleaf: Daybreak at Big Bob Gibson's means time to rekindle the fire and baste the pork.

1920s & 1930s

While repairing a busted railroad tie in **1924, Bob Gibson** contemplated his future with **L&N. With the tension escalating between union workers and the railroad, a major strike and shutdown was looming. The job to which he had devoted twenty years had become less his lifeblood and more an activity to carry him from one weekend barbecue to the next. It was at this time that he worked out his business plan in his head and formed his purpose statement: "Give the people what the people want." Now, this might be eerily similar to Al Capone's philosophy during Prohibition, but it seemed to work for Big Bob through the first couple decades of operation.**

Throughout the 1920s and 1930s, Big Bob's restaurant relocated to different spots all over downtown Decatur, a victim of rent increases, dwindling foot traffic outside the store, changes in riverboat schedules on the Tennessee River, and fluctuating consumer demand. Big Bob knew he was selling what the people craved, but the right location eluded him.

By the beginning of the 1940s, Big Bob had taken the lumps and bruises associated with opening a restaurant and was reaping the rewards of running a successful establishment. Business was good and Big Bob's friendly personality was a magnet for customers. With his increased business he was able to hire a teenaged apprentice named Dutch Drake to work the pitroom while Big Bob told stories and took the customers' money.

Then came World War II and things changed drastically. Money tightened and people were preoccupied with serious thoughts. Business at the restaurant dwindled to a slow trickle that did little more than keep the doors open during these lean years.

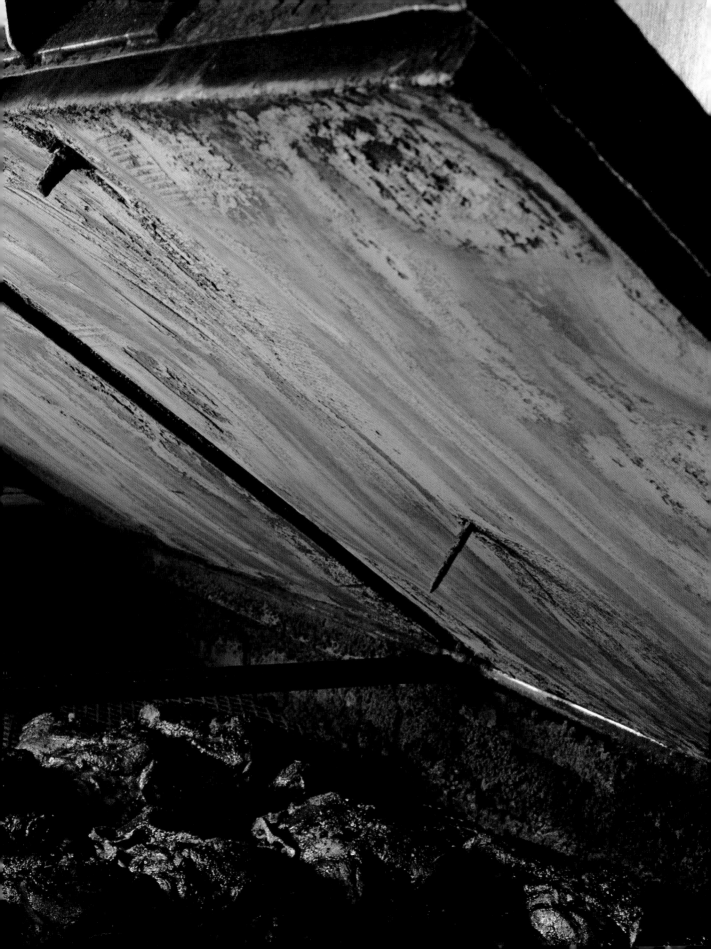

EIGHT-TIME WORLD CHAMPIONSHIP PORK SHOULDER

SERVES: 20 TO 24

COOKING METHOD:
INDIRECT HEAT

SUGGESTED WOOD:
PIGNUT HICKORY

COOKING TIME:
14 TO 16 HOURS

★　★　★　★　★

DRY RUB
½ TABLESPOON DARK BROWN SUGAR

1 TABLESPOON GRANULATED SUGAR

2¼ TEASPOONS GARLIC SALT

2¼ TEASPOONS KOSHER SALT

½ TABLESPOON PAPRIKA

1 TEASPOON CHILI POWDER

⅛ TEASPOON DRIED OREGANO LEAVES

⅛ TEASPOON CAYENNE PEPPER

⅛ TEASPOON GROUND CUMIN

⅛ TEASPOON BLACK PEPPER

INJECTION
¾ CUP APPLE JUICE

½ CUP WATER

½ CUP SUGAR

¼ CUP SALT

2 TABLESPOONS WORCESTERSHIRE SAUCE

1 (16- TO 18-POUND) WHOLE PORK SHOULDER

BIG BOB GIBSON VINEGAR SOP MOP (PAGE 222)

★　★　★　★　★

The whole pork shoulder is exactly that, a hog's entire front haunch. The average shoulder weighs sixteen to twenty pounds and is the shape of a large shoe box. The shoulder is comprised of two different cuts: the "picnic," which is the lower portion and includes the leg bone, and the "butt," which is the top of the shoulder, including the blade bone.

In the barbecue world, restaurant cooking is different from competition cooking. A restaurant customer expects to enjoy a full plate of barbecue and to enjoy the last bite as much as the first. Judges at competitions, on the other hand, usually taste only a bite or two for each entry they are served. If your meat doesn't grab the judges' taste buds and make them whimper with pleasure, the blue ribbon is history. In fact I once heard a master barbecue judge say, "You can't win with good eatin' barbecue."

It is very difficult to walk the fine line between good eatin' and good scorin' 'Q, but this recipe does it. It takes the base flavors and cooking techniques that Big Bob Gibson always used in his restaurant and amplifies them for competition. We add a seasoning blend to enhance the flavor of the bark—the outside crust of the meat—and we use injection to increase the moisture in the pork and permeate the meat throughout with flavorings. We use the same vinegar-based sauce that Big Bob created in the early 1920s to finish the shoulder. These modifications resulted in six straight first place finishes at the Memphis in May World Championship Barbecue Cooking Contest in the pork shoulder category, an added victory at the Jack Daniel's World Championship Invitational Barbecue, and a first place at the largest barbecue contest in the world, the American Royal.

Build a fire (wood or a combination of charcoal and wood) for indirect cooking by situating the coals on only one side of the grill, leaving the other side void.

In a small bowl, combine the dry rub ingredients. Mix well and set aside. In a separate mixing bowl, combine all the injection ingredients and blend until the sugar dissolves. Using a meat syringe, inject the meat evenly at 1-inch intervals from the top side, using the entire amount of the injection solution. Apply the dry rub to the meat in an even coating, patting so the rub adheres.

Recipe continues

When the heat reaches 225°F, place the pork shoulder, skin side down, on the void side of the grill and close the lid. Cook for 14 to 16 hours, adding charcoal as needed during the cooking process to keep the cooker temperature at 225°F. Two small wood chunks should be added every hour to increase the smoke flavor. When the meat has cooked for 13 hours, start basting the shoulder with the vinegar sop mop every hour. When done, the blade bone (the bone visible on the side of the shoulder) should release with a firm tug and the internal temperature of the meat should reach 195°F.

Remove the pork to a cutting board and let it rest for 30 minutes. Wearing insulated rubber gloves, pull the pork from the bones by hand. Pull off and discard all visible fat.

Q: I have a six-foot-long offset smoker which I use for neighborhood parties and church events. The pork I cook turns out great and I always get raves about the moist and tender results. My problem comes when I am cooking a small batch of 'Q for my family. My tough, dry pork gets no love at home!! Help . . .

A: When a cooker is full, more of the meat's natural moisture is trapped within the cooking chamber, creating a more humid cooking environment. This results in moist meat. Try using a smaller cooker for a small batch of 'Q or add water pans to your larger smoker to increase the humidity. Results will be juicy pork and wider smiles.

★ PITMASTER'S TIP ★

Injection is optional, but when done right, it delivers flavor all through the meat right to the bone. Keep in mind that you don't want to overpower the natural flavor of the pork. For the best results, inject the solution evenly throughout the meat from the top side only; this will prevent the liquid from draining out during the cooking process.

PEACH PORK BUTT

SERVES: 10 TO 12

COOKING METHOD:
INDIRECT HEAT

SUGGESTED WOOD:
HICKORY, PEACH, PECAN

COOKING TIME:
7 TO 10 HOURS

★ ★ ★ ★ ★

DRY RUB

1 TABLESPOON DARK BROWN SUGAR

1 TABLESPOON TURBINADO OR RAW SUGAR

1 TABLESPOON PAPRIKA

2¼ TEASPOONS SALT

1 TEASPOON GARLIC SALT

1 TEASPOON BLACK PEPPER

¾ TEASPOON CHILI POWDER

¼ TEASPOON CELERY SALT

¼ TEASPOON GROUND CUMIN

¼ TEASPOON CAYENNE PEPPER

INJECTION

¾ CUP PEACH JUICE (DRAINED FROM THE CANNED PEACHES USED IN THE SAUCE, BELOW)

¼ CUP GRANULATED SUGAR

2 TABLESPOONS SALT

1 TABLESPOON WORCESTERSHIRE SAUCE

1 (6- TO 8-POUND) BONE-IN PORK BUTT

SAUCE

2 CUPS MEMPHIS-STYLE CHAMPIONSHIP RED SAUCE (PAGE 220)

1 CAN PEACHES IN NATURAL JUICES, DRAINED (JUICES RESERVED) AND CHOPPED

★ ★ ★ ★ ★

When you have a craving for pulled pork but a whole shoulder is more meat than you need, the pork butt is your best option. The butt is not the rear end of a pig but the upper portion of the shoulder. This six- to eight-pound cut is usually well marbled and holds up well during long cooks. Most competition barbecue teams select the pork butt when going for the blue ribbon in the pork category because it has more marbling than the picnic portion of the shoulder and is more easily manageable on the grill than the entire shoulder.

I created this recipe for a huge neighborhood block party in Birmingham, Alabama. There are only two things that go together better than a barbecue block party and Birmingham, and that is peaches and pork. If you are ever invited to a barbecue in Alabama, pack your overnight bag.

Build a fire (wood or a combination of charcoal and wood) for indirect cooking by situating the coals on only one side of the grill, leaving the other side void.

In a small bowl, combine the dry rub ingredients. Mix well and set aside. In a separate mixing bowl, combine all the injection ingredients and blend until the sugar dissolves. Using a meat syringe, inject the meat evenly at 1-inch intervals from the top side, using the entire amount of the injection solution. Coat the pork evenly with dry rub, patting gently until the mixture adheres to the meat.

When the heat reaches 250°F, place the pork butt on the void side of the cooker, close the lid, and cook over indirect heat for 7 to 10 hours, until the internal temperature of the pork reaches 190°F. Continually monitor the grill temperature and add hot charcoal or wood coals as needed, to maintain the cooker temperature of 250°F. Remove the pork to a cutting board and let it rest for 20 minutes.

In a saucepan, combine the barbecue sauce and chopped peaches and bring to a simmer over medium heat. Reduce the heat to low and simmer for 10 minutes. Slice, pull, or chop the cooked meat into bite-size pieces and serve drizzled with the sauce or pass the sauce on the side.

CARIBBEAN JERK PORK PICNIC

SERVES: **8 TO 10**

COOKING METHOD:
INDIRECT HEAT

SUGGESTED WOOD:
HICKORY, PECAN, OAK

COOKING TIME:
7 TO 8 HOURS

★ ★ ★ ★ ★

JERK PASTE

1 OR 2 SCOTCH BONNET OR HABANERO PEPPERS, SEEDED

½ CUP DICED ONION

1 GREEN ONION, DICED

1 GARLIC CLOVE, MINCED

½ TABLESPOON SALT

1 TEASPOON GROUND ALLSPICE

1 TEASPOON BLACK PEPPER

¾ TEASPOON DRIED THYME

¼ TEASPOON GROUND GINGER

¼ TEASPOON CINNAMON

¼ TEASPOON GROUND NUTMEG

1 TABLESPOON VEGETABLE OIL

1 5- TO 6-POUND PORK PICNIC

Some of my favorite times away from Big Bob Gibson's have been spent learning the secrets of jerk barbecue in Jamaica. The cooking techniques and flavors of this wonderful Caribbean island are truly unique and magnificent. Scotch bonnet peppers, allspice, onions, garlic, and pimento-wood smoke make Jamaica a barbecue destination. By using these same Caribbean flavors on a pork picnic, which is the lower portion of a pig's shoulder, authentic Jamaican Jerk can be made at home.

If you are lucky enough to visit Jamaica, be sure to get out of the cities and locate any of the well-known jerk shacks scattered over the island. Most Jamaican barbecue joints contain two open-air barbecue pits, one for chicken and another for pork. Cooking pork on the chicken pit is strictly prohibited. A cooking grate made from pimento-wood logs laid side by side is placed directly over a bed of pimento-wood coals; to keep the wood grate from burning, the pitmaster hand turns each log every hour, and the pork or chicken on the cooking grate is covered with a thin sheet of corrugated metal. This simplest of cookers proves that it is not the sophistication of the cooker but the knowledge of the cook that produces the best 'Q!

In 2003, my wife, Amy, and I went to Jamaica to cook in the International Jamaican Jerk Style/Southern Barbecue Cook-Off. Cooking teams from all over the world, including Switzerland, Puerto Rico, Germany, England, the United States, and Jamaica, competed in the event. Each team was given the same raw ingredients: two barrel grills, two chickens, two slabs of ribs, two pork butts, and two red snappers. The chickens were fresh and free range. I use the term "free range" with a bit of sarcasm because these beauties were muscled-up and tough. When holding the ribs up to the sky, beams of sunlight penetrated this thin cut of meat (Jamaican ribs: SPF 15). The cut of pork was unlike any I had ever seen. It contained a portion of the shoulder and of the neck, and it even had four ribs attached. Nonetheless, we were all on an even playing field—or grill.

JERK DIPPING SAUCE

2 CUPS MEMPHIS-STYLE CHAMPIONSHIP
RED SAUCE (PAGE 220)

2 TABLESPOONS RESERVED JERK PASTE

★ ★ ★ ★ ★

We had eighteen hours to prepare our entries and serve them to a group of judges comprised of an equal number of Jamaican and international judges. A "blind" judging procedure was used to score each category. By combining local jerk flavors with cooking techniques learned back home at Big Bob's, we captured the Grand Championship.

Build a fire (wood or a combination of charcoal and wood) for indirect cooking by situating the coals on only one side of the grill, leaving the other side void.

Put all the jerk paste ingredients, except for the oil, into a food processor. Run the processor while adding the oil slowly until a smooth paste forms. Reserve 2 tablespoons of the jerk paste for the dipping sauce. Rub the pork picnic all over with the remaining jerk paste.

When the heat reaches 250°F, place the pork picnic in the cooker, close the lid, and cook over indirect heat for 7 to 8 hours, until the internal temperature of the pork reaches 190°F. Continually monitor the grill temperature and add hot charcoal or wood coals as needed, to maintain the cooker temperature of 250°F. Remove the pork to a cutting board and let it rest for 20 minutes.

In a saucepan, combine the barbecue sauce and reserved jerk paste and bring to a simmer over medium heat. Reduce the heat to low and simmer for 10 minutes. Slice, pull, or chop the cooked meat into bite-size pieces and serve drizzled with the sauce or pass the sauce on the side.

RUBBED AND GRILLED PORK LOIN
with Apple Bourbon Barbecue Sauce

SERVES: 10 TO 16

COOKING METHOD:
DIRECT AND INDIRECT HEAT

SUGGESTED WOOD:
HICKORY, APPLE

COOKING TIME: 2 HOURS

★　★　★　★　★

1 BONELESS PORK TOP LOIN ROAST,
4 TO 5 POUNDS

1 TEASPOON OLIVE OIL

DRY RUB

2 TEASPOONS GRANULATED SUGAR

2 TEASPOONS PAPRIKA

1½ TEASPOONS ONION SALT

1½ TEASPOONS GARLIC SALT

1 TEASPOON GROUND BLACK PEPPER

½ TEASPOON CHILI POWDER

½ TEASPOON GROUND CUMIN

½ TEASPOON GROUND CORIANDER

APPLE BOURBON BARBECUE SAUCE
(PAGE 227)

★　★　★　★　★

Above the shoulder of a pig from the neck to the hams lie the pork loins. Pigs are equipped with two meaty loins located on the top sides of the spine. Buying whole loins will not break your wallet or your waistline. A three-ounce serving contains about one hundred fifty calories with six grams of fat. These loins can be smoked whole, divided into smaller roasts (typically two to five pounds), or cut into pork chops. This cut should not be confused with the pork tenderloin, which is much smaller (three quarters of a pound to one and a half pounds) and is located in the loin area but underneath the rib cage of the pig.

This recipe combines the charring effect of direct grilling and the slow heat of the indirect cooking process to create a tender roast that retains its moisture. I created this recipe for the National Pork Board a few years back. The Apple Bourbon Barbecue Sauce is a sweet complement to the spicy dry rub and smoked flavors. The dish is a nice change from pork chops, which is the traditional use for this cut of meat.

Prepare your grill for direct and indirect heat by building a fire (wood or a combination of charcoal and wood) on one side of the grill, leaving the other side void.

Place the pork loin on a cutting board or platter and brush all over with the oil. In a small bowl, stir together the dry rub seasonings. Apply the dry rub to the meat in an even coating, patting so the rub adheres.

When the cooker reaches 400°F, place the pork loin directly over the medium-hot coals. Cook for 10 minutes on each side to brown. Move the pork away from the heat, cover the grill, and cook for 70 to 90 minutes or until the pork's internal temperature reaches 150°F. Baste with the apple bourbon sauce during the last 10 minutes of cooking. Let the pork loin rest on a cutting board under tented foil for 10 minutes before slicing.

★ PITMASTER'S TIP ★

The internal temperature of most meats, including pork, will spike by at least five degrees after you remove it from the grill. Let it sit or "rest" undisturbed on your counter for 10 to 15 minutes. This rest allows the temperature to equalize and gives the meat fibers time to reabsorb the internal juices. If you can resist digging in, you'll appreciate and enjoy the extra moisture.

GRILLED CHOPS
with Apple-Cranberry Maple Glaze

SERVES: 6

COOKING METHOD:
DIRECT HEAT

SUGGESTED WOOD:
HICKORY, APPLE, APRICOT

BRINING TIME:
12 TO 24 HOURS

COOKING TIME:
16 MINUTES

★　★　★　★　★

BRINE
1½ CUPS APPLE CIDER

1½ CUPS WATER

3½ TABLESPOONS KOSHER SALT

1 TABLESPOON SUGAR

1 TABLESPOON CRACKED BLACK PEPPER

½ TABLESPOON DRIED THYME

½ TEASPOON DRIED MINCED GARLIC

6 DRIED ALLSPICE BERRIES

½ BAY LEAF

6 BONE-IN PORK CHOPS OR BONELESS
LOIN CHOPS (1 INCH THICK)

GLAZE
½ CUP PURE MAPLE SYRUP

½ CUP CRANBERRY SAUCE

½ CUP APPLESAUCE

2 TABLESPOONS SPICY BROWN MUSTARD

¼ TEASPOON SALT

¼ TEASPOON BLACK PEPPER

1/16 TEASPOON CAYENNE PEPPER

★　★　★　★　★

If a whole pork loin or pork loin roast is too large for your needs or will take too long to cook, loin chops are a great alternative. The following recipe qualifies as a "must cook" pork chop. I first made these chops while tailgating in Jupiter, Florida, at the St. Louis Cardinals' spring training facility. March is not too early to start grilling, especially when you are sharing the grill with Hall of Fame shortstop Ozzie Smith! This recipe can be made with either bone-in chops or boneless pork loin cut in one-inch medallions. These pork chops feature apple cider brine and a fruity sweet glaze made from applesauce, cranberry sauce, and maple syrup.

In a large bowl, combine the brine ingredients and stir well. Place the chops in a resealable plastic bag and pour in the brine. Refrigerate for 12 to 24 hours, turning once.

Combine the glaze ingredients in a medium saucepan and mix well. Heat the glaze over medium heat, just until warm. Remove from the heat and reserve ½ cup of glaze for serving.

Build a charcoal and/or wood fire for direct grilling. Grill the chops directly over the hot coals (approximately 450°F) for 8 minutes on each side, or until the internal temperature is 150°F. During the last 3 minutes of cooking, baste both sides of the chops with the glaze. Drizzle the reserved glaze over the chops or pass separately at the table.

SMOKED PORK TENDERLOIN
with Michigan Cherry Glaze

SERVES: 6 TO 8

COOKING METHOD:
INDIRECT HEAT

SUGGESTED WOOD:
HICKORY, CHERRY, OAK

MARINATING TIME:
4 TO 12 HOURS

COOKING TIME:
1 HOUR 30 MINUTES

★ ★ ★ ★ ★

MARINADE

¼ CUP SOY SAUCE

¼ CUP DARK BROWN SUGAR

¼ CUP CHERRY COLA

3 TABLESPOONS OLIVE OIL

1 TEASPOON MINCED ONION

1 TEASPOON GROUND BLACK PEPPER

½ TEASPOON SALT

½ TEASPOON MINCED GARLIC

2 WHOLE PORK TENDERLOINS
(1½ TO 3 POUNDS TOTAL)

GLAZE

6 OUNCES MICHIGAN CHERRY PRESERVES

1 TABLESPOON PURE MAPLE SYRUP

½ TABLESPOON DISTILLED VINEGAR

½ TEASPOON WORCESTERSHIRE SAUCE

1½ TEASPOONS WATER

★ ★ ★ ★ ★

The pork tenderloin has a very mild flavor and because of this, it is a very versatile meat. It is often prepared with a strong, flavorful marinade, dry rub, stuffing, or sauce. This elongated muscle usually weighs between three quarters of a pound and one and a half pounds and can be cooked at either hot or low temperatures. The tenderloin is typically barbecued whole and, when done, cross-cut and served as medallions.

Smoked Pork Tenderloin with Michigan Cherry Glaze begins with a bath in a rich marinade highlighted by cherry cola. Soy and brown sugar provide the depth of flavor, and the cherry cola adds a fruity punch while the acidity of it works to tenderize the meat. The earthy flavor of the smoked pork tenderloin is finished with a sweet glaze made from Michigan cherry preserves. This recipe was created in 2007 for an ESPN/Kingsford game day matchup when this tenderloin was pitted against Joe Theismann's Luck o' the Irish Lamb Chops. It was Michigan against Notre Dame on the field and grill. Here's the winning recipe.

In a large bowl, combine the marinade ingredients and mix well. Place the tenderloins in a resealable plastic bag and pour in the marinade. Refrigerate for 4 to 12 hours.

Build a fire (wood or a combination of charcoal and wood) for indirect cooking by situating the coals on only one side of the grill, leaving the other side void. When the cooker reaches 250°F, place the tenderloins on the void side of the grill and close the lid. Cook for 1 hour and 15 minutes, turning once.

Combine the glaze ingredients in a small bowl. Use a small pastry brush to paint the tenderloins with the glaze. Cook for an additional 10 to 15 minutes, or until the internal temperature of the tenderloins is 155 to 160°F. Let the tenderloins rest under tented foil for 10 minutes on a cutting board, slice into medallions, and serve.

SLAB BACON

COOKING METHOD:
INDIRECT HEAT

SUGGESTED WOOD:
HICKORY, MAPLE, PEACH

COOKING TIME:
1 HOUR 15 MINUTES

* * * * *

2 POUNDS SLAB BACON, UNCURED AND UNSALTED

MUSTARD PASTE

¼ CUP PREPARED MUSTARD

¼ CUP BROWN SUGAR

¼ CUP CHILI POWDER

4 TEASPOONS SALT

1 TEASPOON CAYENNE PEPPER

* * * * *

We normally think of bacon as the thin slices of cured pork found in the aisles of our favorite grocery store or as crispy strips of meat acting as a tasty buffer between our eggs and biscuits in the early morning. The USDA defines bacon as "the cured belly of a swine carcass," but it is more loosely accepted as cuts of meat taken from the belly, sides, or back of a pig.

Big Bob Gibson was fond of bacon not only as a delicious food in its own right, but as part of the cooking process. He would season slab bacon and cook it above leaner cuts of meat such as ham, pork tenderloin, turkey, whole goat, or venison. The meat below the slab bacon would bathe in a shower of hot lard, ensuring a tender, moist, and flavorful result. Big Bob also placed slab bacon in the rib cage of whole pigs while they were cooking on the pit to ensure that the ribs and loin would not overcook while the shoulders and hams of the pig were still roasting. Diced slab bacon also made an occasional appearance in Big Bob's Brunswick stew, baked beans, pinto beans, black-eyed peas, and greens. If Big Bob's regular customers were observant, the aroma of slab bacon was a giveaway that their food would be extra tasty that day.

Slab bacon was a special treat to him because he enjoyed the charred crisp edges. This recipe maximizes the amount of charred caramelized bits by cutting the slab in pieces prior to cooking. It was not a regular menu item, but it showed up when Big Bob wanted to add extra flavor to other foods he was preparing that day. Although Big Bob's favorite slab bacon recipe was never written down, the following recipe comes close to matching his flavors.

With a sharp knife, remove the rind (skin) from the slab bacon. Cut the slab into 1-inch-thick slices, yielding pieces measuring 1 x 1 x 8 inches.

In a small bowl, stir together the ingredients for the mustard paste. Coat each piece of bacon with the paste.

Build a fire (wood or a combination of charcoal and wood) for indirect cooking by situating the coals on only one side of the grill, leaving the other side void. When the cooker reaches 275°F, place the slab bacon on the grill away from the coals and close the lid. Cook for 1 hour and 15 minutes, or until the internal temperature of the bacon reaches 185 to 190°F. Remove and let cool slightly.

Cut the slab bacon into cubes and use it to flavor soups, stews, or side dishes. Extra bacon cubes can be packaged in small quantities and frozen for future recipes.

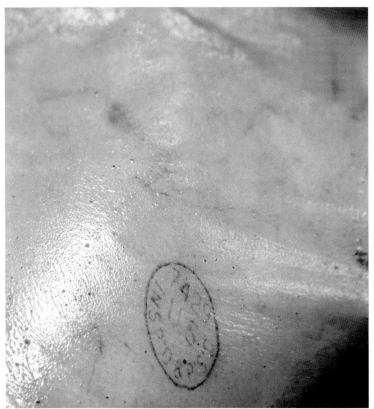

Inspected, stamped, and ready for the pit.

★ PITMASTER'S TIP ★

Most slab bacon is sold with the rind attached. Remove the rind before cooking. If you render the fat from the rind by frying it in a skillet you will produce cracklings, a favorite Southern snack on its own or great as a flavor booster in recipes like cornbread.

BARBECUE BACON-WRAPPED SHRIMP
with Basil Stuffing

SERVES: **6 TO 8**

COOKING METHOD:
INDIRECT HEAT

SUGGESTED WOOD:
HICKORY, APPLE, OAK, MAPLE

COOKING TIME:
17 MINUTES

★ ★ ★ ★ ★

30 BASIL LEAVES, COARSELY CHOPPED

2 TABLESPOONS FRESHLY GRATED PARMESAN CHEESE

1 TEASPOON FRESH MINCED GARLIC

30 LARGE SHRIMP (21–25 COUNT PER POUND), PEELED WITH TAIL SHELLS ON

15 THIN BACON SLICES, CUT IN HALF

SAUCE

1¼ CUPS BARBECUE SAUCE, BOTTLED OR HOMEMADE

¼ CUP APPLESAUCE

¼ CUP PURE MAPLE SYRUP

1 TABLESPOON BALSAMIC VINEGAR

★ ★ ★ ★ ★

I was first given the opportunity to cook at the James Beard Foundation in 2003. It was exciting, because it is a huge honor to be invited to cook at the home of James Beard. My wife, Amy, and I, along with her parents, Don and Carolyn McLemore, came up with a simple plan: We would pull our cooker to New York, set up in front of the Foundation, and cook for a party of eighty to a hundred people. Big Bob Gibson's regularly caters for six thousand to eight thousand people, so this seemed like a slam dunk!

In the South it is not uncommon to drive down a city street and see smoke billowing from a portable cooker. Under a pop-up tent with a handwritten sign reading BBQ PLATE $5.00, you can find the most delicious barbecue you have ever tasted. New York City is a different cut of beef. In order to cook on the street you must first make the police department aware of your intentions and obtain a single-day or multiple-day "festival permit," depending on how long your cooker will stay curbside. This is a tricky process for a bunch of folks from Alabama trying to navigate the system. While waiting for approval we found that the fire department needed to be included in all outdoor cooking discussions. And we couldn't forget to hire a fire marshal to sit with the cooker overnight: safety first.

Although logistics were tedious, the result was flawless. The New York City Police Department met us at the Lincoln Tunnel and gave us an escort to the Foundation. They also blocked off the one-way street in front of the event until we could parallel park at James Beard's front door. Soon after, we were greeted by the fire department, who were not only concerned with fire safety but also with making our stay in the city pleasant. It was then that we realized we needed to cook more food.

For Beard events, it is customary to offer your guests appetizers during the social period prior to dinner service. This is what we served. As always, our logic was, "You can't mess anything up if you wrap it in bacon."

Recipe continues

Mix together the basil, cheese, and garlic. Cut deep down the back of each shrimp and remove the vein. Fill the cut with 1/2 teaspoon of the basil stuffing. Wrap each shrimp with 1/2 slice of bacon and tuck the loose end or secure the bacon with a toothpick, leaving only the shrimp tail exposed.

Build a fire (wood or a combination of charcoal and wood) for indirect cooking by situating the coals on only one side of the grill, leaving the other side void. When the grill temperature reaches 400°F, place the shrimp on the grill away from the coals and with the tails pointing up. Close the lid and cook the shrimp for 14 minutes. Drain the shrimp on a paper-towel-lined platter.

Stir the sauce ingredients together in a small bowl. Holding the shrimp by the tail, dip each into the sauce, and return it to the grill away from the coals. Close the cooker lid and allow the sauce to caramelize (about 3 minutes). Serve hot.

EARLY 1940s

Big Bob's former job with L&N and his experience with metal fabrication made his talents valuable during the war. With a need to make more money and a desire to offer a patriotic hand in the war effort, he moved temporarily to Mobile, Alabama. The shipyards in this port city were his destination, and there he spent two years of his life while his lifeblood remained a faint wisp of smoke in Decatur.

The labor was monotonous but steady and the money was fair. Big Bob's war effort came to a dramatic end one day when he was welding in the bottom of a double-hulled warship. What had been routine work became a nightmare when he turned to exit and realized he had been riveted inside this metal coffin with no way to escape. After countless bellows of rage, he realized his only hope of freedom lay in his hand. As the crowd of workers on the docks gasped, Big Bob Gibson emerged from the steel belly of the ship with a cutting torch held tightly in his grip. He left the shipyard that day with a smile on his face, knowing he was going home to his lifeblood of barbecue.

PIT-FIRED CARIBBEAN PORK TENDERLOIN
with Passion Fruit Butter Sauce

SERVES: 6 TO 8

COOKING METHOD:
INDIRECT HEAT

SUGGESTED WOOD:
HICKORY, OAK, APRICOT

MARINATING TIME:
4 TO 8 HOURS

COOKING TIME:
1 HOUR 20 MINUTES

* * * * *

MARINADE

2 TABLESPOONS OLIVE OIL

2 TABLESPOONS FRESH LIME JUICE

2 TABLESPOONS SOY SAUCE

2 TABLESPOONS APPLE JUICE

2 TABLESPOONS SUGAR

2 TABLESPOONS TOMATO-BASED
BARBECUE SAUCE

3 GARLIC CLOVES, MINCED

½ TABLESPOON DRIED OREGANO

½ TABLESPOON WORCESTERSHIRE SAUCE

½ TABLESPOON DISTILLED VINEGAR

¼ TEASPOON GROUND CUMIN

¼ TEASPOON BLACK PEPPER

¼ TEASPOON CAYENNE PEPPER

2 WHOLE PORK TENDERLOINS
(1½ TO 3 POUNDS TOTAL)

PASSION FRUIT BUTTER SAUCE (PAGE 233)

* * * * *

Through changes in breeding and feed, today's commodity pork cuts are 16 percent leaner and have 27 percent less saturated fat than those of just fifteen years ago. In my humble opinion, this might be a little too lean. Lower fat means less flavor and moisture within the meat. Regardless, one of my favorite cuts of meat for the charcoal grill is still the pork tenderloin. This lean cut has fewer than three grams of fat for a three-ounce serving; that's as lean as a skinless chicken breast. Sometimes the pig doesn't get the love it deserves, you know?

To highlight the versatility of pork tenderloin, I served this recipe, inspired by my extensive travels in the Caribbean, the first time I cooked for the James Beard Foundation in New York City. Although I served it as an appetizer right off the grill, it also makes a wonderful main course. It combines some of my favorite Southern barbecue flavors with the traditional acidic punch of the food of the islands.

In a large bowl, stir together all the marinade ingredients. Place the tenderloins in a resealable plastic bag and pour in the marinade. Refrigerate for 4 to 8 hours.

Build a fire (wood or a combination of charcoal and wood) for indirect cooking by situating the coals on only one side of the grill, leaving the other side void. When the cooker reaches 250°F, place the tenderloins on the grill away from the fire and close the lid. Cook for 1 hour and 15 minutes, or until the internal temperature of the tenderloins reaches 150 to 155°F. Remove the tenderloins to a platter and cover with foil.

Immediately open the dampers on the grill. When the temperature of the cooker reaches 350°F, close the dampers slightly to maintain that temperature. Drizzle the meat with the Passion Fruit Butter Sauce and return to the grill for 5 minutes; reserve some of the sauce to baste the meat during the cook. Remove the tenderloins from the grill and let them rest for 10 minutes on a cutting board, slice into medallions, and serve.

PECAN-CRUSTED PORK TENDERLOIN PINWHEELS
with Carolina Mustard Sauce

SERVES: 6

COOKING METHOD:
DIRECT HEAT

SUGGESTED WOOD:
HICKORY, PECAN

COOKING TIME:
16 MINUTES

★ ★ ★ ★ ★

1 PORK TENDERLOIN

6 BACON STRIPS

CAROLINA MUSTARD SAUCE (PAGE 228)

1 CUP FINELY CHOPPED PECANS

1 TEASPOON SALT

½ TEASPOON BLACK PEPPER

★ ★ ★ ★ ★

These pinwheels were developed in the kitchens at Big Bob Gibson Bar-B-Q as a part of a campaign for the National Pork Board. This is not your typical "low and slow" barbecue recipe, but rather an "ode to pork," a direct-grilled recipe that features both pork tenderloin **and** pork bacon. Add some pecans and a traditional Carolina mustard sauce and you have an appetizer or entrée with true Southern flair.

Cut the tenderloin lengthwise into 6 long strips approximately ¼ inch thick. Lay the slices on a cutting board; they should be the same size and shape as the bacon strips. Place a strip of bacon on top of each piece of tenderloin. Starting at one end, roll the tenderloin into a pinwheel medallion. Secure with two toothpicks.

Set aside 1 cup of the Carolina Mustard Sauce and apply remaining sauce to the outside of the pinwheels. Stir together the pecans, salt, and pepper, and coat the tenderloin pinwheels with the pecan mixture. Cut each of the pinwheels through the equator to make two thin pinwheel medallions.

Build a charcoal and/or wood fire for direct grilling. Place the medallions on the grill over medium-high heat (375 to 400°F) and cook for 7 to 8 minutes on each side or until the edges of the bacon start to crisp. Serve with the reserved sauce drizzled over each pinwheel.

Q: I always hear people talk about how great the pork tenderloin is. I have tried cooking it both "low and slow" and directly over charcoal, and it always comes out dry. What am I doing wrong?

A: Like all lean cuts of meat, the tenderloin has much less fat available to keep it moist when cooking. This means the window of ideal doneness is much smaller than for fatty meats. Whether you are cooking over direct or indirect heat, making sure you pull your tenderloin off the grill at the right time by using an internal meat thermometer is the key to success. You can't go wrong if you remove your tenderloin from the heat when it registers 155 to 160°F.

Whole pork tenderloin is cut into ¼-inch strips, rolled with bacon, painted with mustard sauce, coated with pecans, and then sliced into medallions. These pinwheel medallions are a grill-ready appetizer or entrée.

CRISP SPICY SOUTHERN MUSTARD COLESLAW

SERVES: 8 TO 10

★ ★ ★ ★ ★

8 CUPS SHREDDED GREEN CABBAGE

1¾ CUPS SHREDDED WHITE ONION

1 CUP SHREDDED GREEN BELL PEPPER

⅓ CUP SHREDDED CARROT

¼ CUP SHREDDED CELERY

⅔ CUP SUGAR

DRESSING

6 TABLESPOONS APPLE CIDER VINEGAR

6 TABLESPOONS YELLOW PREPARED MUSTARD

¼ CUP KETCHUP

¼ CUP SOUR CREAM

2 TABLESPOONS MAYONNAISE

½ TABLESPOON SALT

¼ TEASPOON CAYENNE PEPPER

★ ★ ★ ★ ★

When it comes to side dishes, Big Bob felt keeping it simple was the way to go. Consequently you won't find a long list of accompaniments to choose from on our menu, just potato salad, slaw, baked beans, and potato chips. His original vinegar-based coleslaw (see page 176), made from only four ingredients, was the only slaw that was ever used in the restaurant.

In 2003, Martha Stewart wanted to feature some of our favorite Southern-style sides on her television show and requested both baked bean and slaw recipes. We happily sent her recipes for half the side dishes on our menu. The next day we learned the show preferred we give them a "customary" mustard-based slaw typical of the Memphis Barbecue Region. I'd never heard of such a slaw, but who can argue with Martha Stewart? Thus was Crisp Spicy Southern Mustard Coleslaw born. The recipe has since been served to raves at the James Beard Foundation in New York City and at the South Beach Wine and Food Festival.

Combine the cabbage, onion, bell pepper, carrot, celery, and sugar in a large bowl and mix well. In a separate bowl combine the dressing ingredients and blend until smooth. Pour the dressing over the cabbage mixture and stir together. Chill and serve.

TURNIP GREENS
with Smoked Slab Bacon

SERVES: **6 TO 8**

COOKING TIME:
1 HOUR 15 MINUTES

* * * * *

2 POUNDS TURNIP GREENS
(COLLARD OR MUSTARD GREENS CAN
BE SUBSTITUTED OR MIXED)

½ POUND SMOKED SLAB BACON
(SEE PAGE 66)

5 CUPS WATER

½ CUP DICED ONIONS

2 GARLIC CLOVES, MINCED

2 TABLESPOONS CIDER VINEGAR

1½ TEASPOONS SALT

¼ TEASPOON BLACK PEPPER

⅛ TEASPOON CRUSHED RED PEPPER FLAKES

JUST ADD GREENS PEPPER SAUCE (PAGE 234)

* * * * *

Big Bob always had a standing policy at his restaurant that when you were on the clock you ate for free. Some companies give their staff stock options; Big Bob always gave his staff real Southern fixings. Many staples of the staff meals were not offered to the customers and it was not uncommon to walk into his restaurant and smell fried chicken, sweet potatoes, or catfish cooking. Thank God hickory smoke usually trumped any other aroma or Big Bob Gibson Bar-B-Q might have turned into Big Bob's Southern Kitchen.

While turnip greens have never graced the menu at Big Bob Gibson Bar-B-Q, they were cooked almost as often as any side dish on the menu. Always made with the restaurant's smoked slab bacon, this recipe showcases the simple delight of seasoned greens. Pair them with black-eyed peas, fried potatoes, and cornbread to taste a typical employee meal in Big Bob's kitchen.

Wash the turnip greens in cold water and drain well. Repeat the process twice, making sure all sandy grit is removed from the leaves. Cut off and discard the tough stems and any discolored greens.

Place the bacon in a medium stockpot with the water. Bring to a boil and cook at a rapid simmer. Gradually add the greens, stirring to wilt before adding another batch, until all the greens are in the pot. Add the remaining ingredients and mix well. Reduce the heat to medium-low, cover, and simmer for 1 hour, or until the greens are tender.

Top each serving of greens with a few dashes of pepper sauce or serve the sauce on the side.

STACKED CORNBREAD VEGETABLE SALSA SALAD

SERVES: 8 TO 10

COOKING TIME: 15 MINUTES

★ ★ ★ ★ ★

CORNBREAD

1 TABLESPOON VEGETABLE OIL

3 CUPS BUTTERMILK

2 EGGS

2 CUPS YELLOW CORNMEAL

1 TEASPOON BAKING SODA

1 TEASPOON BAKING POWDER

1 TEASPOON SALT

4 OUNCES CHOPPED JALAPEÑO PEPPER, SEEDS AND RIBS REMOVED (OPTIONAL)

SALAD

1 POUND BACON

1 PACKAGE RANCH-STYLE DRESSING MIX

8 OUNCES SOUR CREAM

1 CUP MAYONNAISE

3 TOMATOES, CHOPPED

½ CUP CHOPPED GREEN BELL PEPPER

½ CUP CHOPPED GREEN ONIONS

2 16-OUNCE CANS PINTO BEANS, DRAINED AND RINSED

3 CUPS SHREDDED CHEDDAR CHEESE

1 15-OUNCE CAN WHOLE KERNEL CORN, DRAINED

★ ★ ★ ★ ★

Memphis in May is a barbecue competition that takes place the third weekend of May at Tom Lee Park on the Mississippi River. It is the largest pork cookoff in the world and is often called "The Super Bowl of Swine." The Big Bob Gibson Competition Cooking Team has attended this contest since 1997 and to date we have never finished out of the top ten. We've won the pork shoulder category six times, won first place in sauce three times, and won the Grand Championship twice. But it is not our success in the competition that stirs the fondest memories of this event; it is the time spent with friends and family while enjoying the relaxing atmosphere.

It is a tradition for us to put on a big feed the Friday night before the most serious part of the competition begins. Our menu changes year to year but almost always includes pork tenderloin, bean salad, homemade pies, and this stacked cornbread vegetable salsa salad. I am not sure where this recipe originally came from, but my mother-in-law, Carolyn McLemore, and her friend Joyce Terry always treat us to a big batch at this annual event. It's good and it goes really well with smoked pork tenderloin.

Preheat the oven to 450°F. Coat the bottom and sides of a 10-inch cast-iron skillet with the vegetable oil and place in the oven to heat. In a medium bowl, combine the buttermilk and eggs and stir. Add the cornmeal, baking soda, baking powder, salt, and jalapeño pepper while stirring briskly. Pour the batter into the hot skillet. Bake for 15 minutes, or until lightly browned. Let cool.

While the cornbread bakes, fry the bacon in a skillet over medium-high heat until crisp. Drain well on paper towels. When cool, crumble into small pieces.

In a medium bowl, combine the ranch dressing mix, sour cream, and mayonnaise and mix well. In another bowl, combine the tomatoes, bell pepper, and green onions to form a chunky salsa. Crumble the cooled cornbread and place half in the bottom of a large serving bowl. Top with half of the pinto beans. Layer half of the salsa mixture over the beans. Follow with half of the cheese, bacon, and corn, and top with half of the dressing. Make a second layer, ending with the dressing. Cover and chill for at least 2 hours before serving.

While Bob Gibson excelled in the pits, Big Mama was at home baking fresh bread and cake in her kitchen.

BIG MAMA'S APPLE NUT CAKE

SERVES: 8 TO 10

COOKING TIME:
1 HOUR 15 MINUTES

★ ★ ★ ★ ★

3 CUPS ALL-PURPOSE FLOUR

2 CUPS SUGAR

1 TEASPOON GROUND CINNAMON

1 TEASPOON BAKING SODA

4 EGGS, LIGHTLY BEATEN

1½ CUPS VEGETABLE OIL

2 CUPS PEELED, GRATED APPLES

1 CUP CHOPPED NUTS

2 TEASPOONS PURE VANILLA EXTRACT

★ ★ ★ ★ ★

Pork is a natural pairing for anything apple. More like a slightly sweet bread than a dessert, Big Mama's Apple Nut Cake is perfect with any pork main course, although it can also be served to end the meal. It can be made either in a loaf pan or in a traditional tube pan, depending on how you plan to serve it.

The spiced fruit aroma this cake emits made it one of Big Mama's favorites. With six kids and Big Bob to look after, she was entitled to a little aromatherapy. Because it was not overly sweet, the kids were allowed to snack on it during the day.

After viewing this recipe I asked Ruth, the youngest daughter of the Gibson clan, what kind of nuts should be used. She said the nut of choice was either hicka nuts or scaly barks, two varieties you are unlikely to find at your local grocer. "Hicka nuts" is turn-of-the-century Southern country slang for hickory nuts, and "scaly barks" are the nut from the shagbark hickory tree. Hickory nuts are tough to crack, and getting the meat out is very difficult, but they must be superior in flavor because Big Mama would walk past three pecan trees to get to the scaly barks. You can substitute whatever nut you prefer.

Preheat the oven to 300°F. Grease a 10 x 5-inch loaf pan or a 10-cup tube pan. In a medium bowl, combine the flour, sugar, cinnamon, and baking soda and mix well. Stir together the eggs and oil and then add to the dry ingredients. Stir in the apples, nuts, and vanilla extract. Pour the mixture into the prepared pan. Bake for 1 hour and 15 minutes before testing the cake for doneness. Remove it from the oven when the cake tester comes out clean. Let the cake cool slightly before removing it from the pan.

BEEF:
BIG
AND
BOLD

★ ★ ★ ★ ★

ALTHOUGH BEEF IS A STAPLE FOOD TODAY, CATTLE ARE

not indigenous to America. It was not until the eighteenth century that Spanish and French colonists began to raise cattle. These cattle farms were confined to very few specific areas of the west, especially near San Antonio. In the early 1800s, western farmers used live cattle drives seeking markets in the popular East. Distribution of beef was accomplished by live cattle transport via the developing railroad system in the 1850s.

When refrigerated railway cars were taken west in 1871, the beef industry was transformed. Large cuts of meat were much easier than live animals to ship, and slaughterhouses sprang up across the Midwest to address the developing appetite for beef in the East.

After the Second World War, the popularity of beef skyrocketed, and by 1952 the average American was eating sixty-two pounds of beef per year, an edible symbol of American prosperity.

★ ★ ★ ★ ★

Beef has remained a staple part of the American diet, and the tradition of cooking cuts of beef in an outdoor barbecue grill is more popular than ever. Thanks to the great state of Texas, any time you mention barbecue and beef in the same sentence, brisket comes to mind. Fresh brisket, cut from the breast or lower chest, was once considered an inexpensive, tough cut of meat and was generally set aside to be ground.

Not until the early to mid-1900s was the process of cooking barbecue brisket as we know it today developed. Some stories credit two German brothers who decided to try slow-smoking brisket alongside their sausages. Rave reviews convinced them to add this new item to the market menu. Other old-timers tell of a brisket that was accidentally left in a covered cooker as its hot fire gradually cooled down, turning into slow-burning coals. What was discovered in the morning was a tender and flavorful piece of beef. Regardless of its genesis, we know today that even the toughest cuts can be made palatable through the slow-cooking process. These results are achieved by breaking down the collagen in the connective muscle tissues, yielding tenderness. "Collagen" and "connective tissue"—are you hungry yet?

In the 1940s, while Texans were perfecting their beef brisket artistry, Bob Gibson decided to develop his own way of introducing beef to Alabama. He selected not the toughest cut of beef, but the largest and one of the leanest pieces, the beef top round. The leanness of this cut appealed to Big Bob because he knew he would get a higher yield of useable meat. He also theorized that a larger piece of meat would hold its moisture for a longer period of time than a small, thin cut like brisket, so he could cook the beef overnight and hold it hot during the day without drying it out. As an added bonus, the price per pound was quite modest. Believe me when I say Big Bob would have cooked the cow whole if the price had been low enough and he could fit the cow in his cooker.

Today beef is one of the more versatile meats and among the tastiest. Whether you choose to adopt the "low and slow" methods of cooking brisket and beef top round or intensify the heat and cook flank steak and tri-tip, this chapter is filled with the tried-and-true instructions. Recipes from the mid-1900s to more recent award-winning beef dishes are listed, featuring cooking techniques commonly used in California, Alabama, and, of course, Texas.

Above and opposite: Big Bob Gibson was bigger than life itself; throughout his life fishing was the one thing that compared closely to the enjoyment he got from barbecuing.

1940s

Toward the end of the war, in 1944, Bob Gibson returned from the shipyards of Mobile. He moved his restaurant from downtown Decatur, Alabama, to Highway 67 on the outskirts of the city, a step back from his earlier larger downtown location. The new place featured four tables and a counter for the customers and only a 4 x 8-foot barbecue pit in the kitchen. The modest scale of the new place was intentional; it seems that selling too much barbecue cut into Big Bob's quality time on the Tennessee River with his fishing rod.

Despite the size of the restaurant and Bob Gibson's desire to cast more and cook less, business at the new location flourished. Barbecue beef was the newest item on the menu, which pleased both regulars and new customers alike. The front end of the restaurant quickly became standing room only, and traffic was almost more than the two employees could manage. Bob Gibson handled the money and worked with his young apprentice, Dutch Drake, in the pitroom. Mattie Johnson took the orders and kept the customers happy.

From the outside, the process of barbecuing seems simple. A limited menu and very few ingredients coupled with lines of customers at the door are an enticing combination for wannabe restaurateurs. This was the situation in 1949 when Big Bob's restaurant and the surrounding property was sold out from under him. The new landowner informed Big Bob that his lease was terminated. Folks who witnessed this event recalled that if this young entrepreneur had been a little slower he would have been terminated as well.

In a rage Bob Gibson left that day with an uncertain future. The only consolation was that the crappie were on beds in the Tennessee River and the larger ones were ravenous that time of year. On his way to the boat launch he passed by a building for sale less than one mile from his former location. With a big grin he made his first cast and immediately felt a strong jerk of the rod. The day had suddenly gotten better.

It was four months later that Big Bob made the move to his new location farther down the highway. He dragged his feet moving out of his old building, and at the same time he coordinated the fastest restaurant transformation in history. His timing was perfect. Big Bob welcomed his customers back the same day the new owner of the old location hung an OPEN sign on his investment. Three weeks later his grin broadened when only one of the two restaurants was still serving barbecue.

BEEF BURNT ENDS

SERVES: 4

**COOKING METHOD:
INDIRECT HEAT**

**SUGGESTED WOOD:
HICKORY, OAK, MESQUITE**

**COOKING TIME:
1 HOUR 30 MINUTES**

★　★　★　★　★

1 SLOW-SMOKED BEEF BRISKET POINT
(SEE PAGE 89) WITH DRIPPINGS

¼ CUP BARBECUE SAUCE, BOTTLED OR
HOMEMADE

★　★　★　★　★

Burnt ends are the charred end pieces and flavorful crumbles that are left in the pooled juices and drippings after a beef brisket has been sliced. I consider them the most flavorful part of the brisket. Usually it's the early bird who gets the worm, but in the case of brisket, it is the last person in line who gets to scrape the cutting board. Burnt ends have become so popular that people have come up with ways to make more of these flavorful brisket bits.

Trim excess fat from the top and bottom of the cooked brisket point.

Build a fire (wood or a combination of charcoal and wood) for indirect cooking by situating the coals on only one side of the grill, leaving the other side void. When the cooker reaches 250°F, place the beef brisket point on the void side of the grill and close the lid. Cook for 1 hour and 30 minutes. Remove the brisket point from the cooker and cut it into bite-size chunks.

In a small pan, mix ½ cup of the beef drippings with the barbecue sauce and heat. Pour the liquid over the beef chunks and serve.

★ PITMASTER'S TIP ★

Rather than view brisket as one cut of meat, think of it as *two* cuts. Within each whole brisket there is the flat and the point. The sliced flat is what most people think of as beef brisket, a very lean muscle with a distinct grain. The point, however, is highly marbled and covered by a thick slab of fat. A thin layer of fat also separates the two cuts. Following this line of fat with a knife allows the flat and point to be separated easily after cooking. With a little extra cook time, the entire point of the brisket can be transformed into those wonderful bites called burnt ends.

BIG BOB GIBSON'S HEAD OF BEEF

SERVES: 60

COOKING METHOD:
INDIRECT HEAT

SUGGESTED WOOD:
HICKORY

COOKING TIME:
16 HOURS

★ ★ ★ ★ ★

1 WHOLE BEEF TOP ROUND
(APPROXIMATELY 30 POUNDS)

SALT

PEPPER

BIG BOB GIBSON BAR-B-Q VINEGAR SOP MOP
(PAGE 222)

★ ★ ★ ★ ★

"Head of beef" is a term that Big Bob used to describe his favorite cut of beef, the top round. This lean cut is taken from the top portion of the back leg and weighs around thirty pounds. When Big Bob began serving top round in the restaurant, he raised his pit lids to the ten-inch clearance needed to fit this enormous hunk of beef into his cooker.

With a sixteen-hour cook time, Big Bob's head of beef roasts slowly overnight on the pit next to the pork shoulders. This gives the simple seasonings time to meld with the natural flavor of the beef. Two things are needed when trying Big Bob's original beef recipe at home: a sturdy grill and a large crowd!

Double a large piece of aluminum foil and place the beef in the center, fat side down. Pour 2 cups of water over the beef while lifting the edges of the foil to trap the water. Season the beef generously with salt and pepper. Wrap the aluminum foil tightly to cover the beef. Cut a three-inch square hole in the top of the foil (this will allow the smoke to flavor the meat while the foil traps the moisture and juices).

Build a fire in the cooker with sticks of hickory. Burn the wood until a bed of coals is created. Add logs to the coals as needed to reach and maintain a temperature of 250°F. Place the wrapped beef in the cooker and cook over indirect heat for 16 hours. When the beef is tender and reaches an internal temperature of 190°F, peel the top of the foil back and mop the beef with Big Bob Gibson Bar-B-Q Vinegar Sop Mop.

Let the meat rest undisturbed in the foil for 1 to 2 hours before serving.

★ PITMASTER'S TIP ★

Placing whole logs on top of a bed of coals is referred to as "banking the fire." This extends cook times at a low temperature and especially comes in handy when no one will be around to tend the fire. Laying logs directly on top of coals prevents air from circulating under the wood and creating large flames, which would make the wood burn too fast. Banking the fire will cause the logs to smolder and hold a steady low temperature all day or night.

SLOW-SMOKED BEEF BRISKET

SERVES: 10 TO 14

COOKING METHOD:
INDIRECT HEAT

SUGGESTED WOOD:
HICKORY, OAK, MESQUITE

COOKING TIME:
9 TO 10 HOURS

★   ★   ★   ★   ★

WET RUB

8 BEEF BOUILLON CUBES

1 TABLESPOON WORCESTERSHIRE SAUCE

1 WHOLE BEEF BRISKET (10 TO 12 POUNDS)

DRY RUB

½ TABLESPOON SALT

½ TABLESPOON PAPRIKA

½ TABLESPOON BLACK PEPPER

½ TABLESPOON SUGAR

¾ TEASPOON GARLIC POWDER

½ TEASPOON ONION POWDER

¼ TEASPOON DRIED OREGANO

⅛ TEASPOON GROUND CORIANDER

★   ★   ★   ★   ★

The following brisket recipe was developed over a period of three years specifically for cooking competitions. It began after learning the requirements of the Kansas City Barbecue Association's competition cooking circuit. I made a trip to my favorite Alabama butcher and asked to see the beef brisket. He proudly told me he had the largest selection of that particular cut in the area. The four varieties of corned beef looked good, but they were not exactly what I was looking for. It seemed we both had a little to learn about barbecue beef brisket.

Many years and tears later I fell in love with the rich beef flavor of this recipe. In the restaurant we serve our brisket as thin slices with the juices drizzled over the fresh cuts of beef, but in competitions we separate the flat from the point and reserve the cooked point to make burnt ends (see page 86). Brisket has become one of our most consistent categories in cooking competitions, including wins at the American Royal Invitational Contest in Kansas City, Missouri, and the Best of the Best Invitational BBQ Cook-off in Douglas, Georgia.

Build a fire (wood or a combination of charcoal and wood) for indirect cooking by situating the coals on only one side of the grill, leaving the other side void.

Crush the beef bouillon cubes in a small bowl and mix with the Worcestershire. Cover the entire brisket with the wet rub. In a small bowl, mix the dry rub ingredients, then coat the brisket with the dry rub.

When the cooker reaches 225°F, place the beef brisket, with the fat side up, on the void side of the grill and close the lid. Cook for 7 to 8 hours, until the internal temperature of the brisket reaches 160 to 170°F. Two small wood chunks should be added every hour to increase the smoke flavor.

Fold a large piece of aluminum foil in half and place the brisket in the center, fat side down. Pour 1 cup of water over the brisket while lifting the edges of the foil to trap the water. Bring the foil edges together and fold, wrapping the entire brisket tight, and place in the cooker for an additional 2 hours, until the internal temperature of the brisket reaches 185 to 190°F.

Let the meat rest in the foil undisturbed for 1 to 2 hours. Remove the brisket from the foil and slice across the grain. Save the beef juices collected in the foil to drizzle over the brisket slices.

BARE NAKED BRISKET

SERVES: 10 TO 14

COOKING METHOD:
INDIRECT HEAT

SUGGESTED WOOD:
HICKORY, OAK

COOKING TIME:
8 TO 10 HOURS

★ ★ ★ ★ ★

SEASONING PASTE

2 TABLESPOONS BROWN SUGAR

2 TABLESPOONS KOSHER SALT

2 TABLESPOONS PAPRIKA

2 TABLESPOONS WORCESTERSHIRE SAUCE

1 TABLESPOON PREPARED MUSTARD

1 TABLESPOON ONION POWDER

1 TABLESPOON BLACK PEPPER

2 TEASPOONS CAYENNE PEPPER

4 GARLIC CLOVES, MINCED

1 WHOLE BEEF BRISKET (10 TO 12 POUNDS)

★ ★ ★ ★ ★

There are both pros and cons to wrapping meat during the cooking process. Kansas City pitmaster Paul Kirk has often referred to the process of wrapping your meat with foil during cooking as the "Texas crutch." He maintains that wrapping is not needed to get tender, flavorful barbecue. Cooking in foil can dilute the barbecue flavors you have worked very hard to put into your meat, washing away the smoke flavor and natural caramelization of barbecue meat. The longer food stays in foil, the more it is cooked by steam. The obvious advantage to wrapping with foil is that the meat becomes more tender, but another plus is capturing the natural juices. These juices can later be drizzled over the barbecue or mixed with sauce to add an extra flair to your barbecue. Either cooking method can produce amazing results.

For those who want to simplify the cooking process or retain maximum smoke flavor, this recipe is ideal. It utilizes a seasoning paste to flavor the beef. The paste will adhere to the brisket nicely during the smoking process, ensuring a great taste. No foil, no problem. Paul, this one's for you.

In a small bowl, combine the seasoning paste ingredients and mix well. Smear the entire brisket with the paste until evenly coated.

Build a fire (wood or a combination of charcoal and wood) for indirect cooking by situating the coals on only one side of the grill, leaving the other side void. When the cooker reaches 225°F, place the beef brisket on the void side of the grill and close the lid. Cook for 8 to 10 hours, until the internal temperature of the brisket reaches 185 to 190°F. Remove the brisket to a pan and cover.

Let the meat rest in the pan covered for 1 hour. Slice the brisket across the grain of the meat and serve.

SCALLOP BURNT ENDS

SERVES: 6 (2 SCALLOPS PER SERVING)

COOKING METHOD: DIRECT HEAT

SUGGESTED WOOD: OAK, ALDER

COOKING TIME: 6 TO 8 MINUTES

★ ★ ★ ★ ★

DRY RUB

½ TABLESPOON SALT

½ TABLESPOON PAPRIKA

½ TABLESPOON BLACK PEPPER

½ TABLESPOON SUGAR

¾ TEASPOON GARLIC POWDER

½ TEASPOON ONION POWDER

¼ TEASPOON DRIED OREGANO

⅛ TEASPOON GROUND CORIANDER

12 SEA SCALLOPS

12 SLICES FULLY COOKED BEEF BRISKET (PREFERABLY FROM THE POINT)

RESERVED BEEF DRIPPINGS

★ ★ ★ ★ ★

Here's a barbecue-style surf and turf! This recipe combines both barbecuing and grilling techniques, with slow-cooked brisket slices wrapped around fresh scallops and cooked on a hot grill. Our tasty way to use up leftover brisket slices was featured on **Live with Regis and Kelly** in 2007. Serve it hot off the grill as either an appetizer or a main course.

In a small bowl, combine the dry rub ingredients and mix well.

Remove the small adductor muscle from the side of each scallop. Wrap each scallop with a slice of brisket and secure with a wooden toothpick. Season the exposed scallop lightly with the dry rub.

Build a charcoal and/or wood fire for direct grilling. Apply a light coat of oil to the grill grate. Grill the scallops directly over the hot coals (approximately 400°F) while basting with reserved beef drippings. Cook for 3 to 4 minutes on each side until the scallop slightly firms or the internal temperature is 130°F.

PEPPER-AND-HERB-CRUSTED FLANK STEAK

SERVES: 6 TO 8

COOKING METHOD:
DIRECT HEAT

SUGGESTED WOOD:
HICKORY, OAK, MESQUITE

MARINATING TIME:
2 TO 12 HOURS

COOKING TIME:
10 MINUTES

★　★　★　★　★

PEPPER AND HERB SEASONING

¼ CUP FRESH THYME LEAVES, MINCED

2 TABLESPOONS FRESH TARRAGON LEAVES, MINCED

1 TABLESPOON FRESH ROSEMARY LEAVES, MINCED

2 TABLESPOONS COARSELY GROUND BLACK PEPPER

4 GARLIC CLOVES, MINCED FINE

2 TEASPOONS SALT

2 TEASPOONS DARK BROWN SUGAR

1 TEASPOON CRUSHED RED PEPPER FLAKES

2 TEASPOONS EXTRA-VIRGIN OLIVE OIL

2 TEASPOONS SOY SAUCE

2 FLANK STEAKS, APPROXIMATELY 2 POUNDS EACH

★　★　★　★　★

Flank steak is the only steak that comprises a single large muscle. It is located in the underbelly muscles of a cow, between the rib and the hip. This oval-shaped cut ranges from 1 to 1½ pounds and is long, thin, and very fibrous. Select a bright red flank steak that has plenty of marbling.

If prepared incorrectly, flank steak is one of the toughest cuts of beef, but when cooked properly it is one of the best-tasting grilled meats. The large, thin cut results in more surface area to form a flavorful bark. The secrets to cooking a great flank steak are grilling quickly over a hot fire and slicing the meat across the grain.

One of the most popular ways to flavor meat is marination. However, a marinade doesn't need to be liquid to be effective; the same effect can be achieved with a dry rub or a paste rather than a highly seasoned liquid. In this recipe a long soak in a blend of fresh herbs and seasonings makes the thin steak explode with flavor.

Combine the pepper and herb seasoning ingredients together in a small bowl and mix well to form a coarse paste. Spread the paste evenly over both sides of each flank steak. Wrap the flank steaks individually with plastic wrap and refrigerate for 2 to 12 hours.

Build a charcoal and/or wood fire for direct grilling. Grill the steaks directly over the coals (approximately 450 to 500°F) for 5 minutes on each side, until an internal temperature of 135 to 145°F is reached for medium-rare to medium doneness.

Let the meat rest under tented foil for 10 to 15 minutes. For optimum tenderness, cut the flank steaks across the grain into ¼-inch-thick slices and serve.

GRILLED SOY AND LIME BEEF TRI-TIP

SERVES: 6 TO 8

COOKING METHOD:
DIRECT AND INDIRECT HEAT

SUGGESTED WOOD:
HICKORY, OAK, MESQUITE

MARINATING TIME:
4 TO 12 HOURS

COOKING TIME:
40 MINUTES

★ ★ ★ ★ ★

MARINADE

1½ CUPS APPLE JUICE

¼ CUP SOY SAUCE

3 TABLESPOONS SEASONED SALT

3 TABLESPOONS DARK CORN SYRUP

2½ TABLESPOONS FRESH LIME JUICE

1 TABLESPOON CRUSHED RED PEPPER FLAKES

2 TEASPOONS WORCESTERSHIRE SAUCE

1½ TEASPOONS MSG (OPTIONAL)

1 TEASPOON MINCED GARLIC

¼ TEASPOON CAYENNE PEPPER

¼ TEASPOON GROUND GINGER

1 BEEF TRI-TIP (APPROXIMATELY 2½ POUNDS)
2 BEEF BOUILLON CUBES

★ ★ ★ ★ ★

The tri-tip comes from the bottom sirloin, located just forward of the back leg on the outside belly of the cow. This small cut of beef weighs between 1½ and 2½ pounds and is two inches thick. In Europe this cut of beef is sometimes referred to as a "triangle steak," because of its shape.

In the past, butchers seldom marketed this obscure cut because there were only two small tri-tips per beef carcass. Typically it was ground or cubed for stews. But because it is lean and inexpensive it has recently become quite popular, especially on the West Coast.

One of the most popular items at a California cookout is the beef tri-tip. Telling a Californian that grilling a beef tri-tip is not real barbecue may lead to fisticuffs. This cut packs big flavor, but it has a low fat content. For optimum taste, tri-tip is usually marinated and/or seasoned and grilled at a high temperature over direct heat. The tenderness of this cut is optimized by slicing the meat across the grain. This recipe stays true to the flavors of the West Coast.

In a shallow baking dish or resealable plastic bag, combine the marinade ingredients and mix well. Add the beef and cover or seal. Marinate in the refrigerator for 4 to 12 hours.

When ready to cook, grind the beef bouillon cubes into a powder. Remove the tri-tip from the marinade, discard the marinade, and pat the meat dry. Sprinkle the meat evenly with the bouillon powder and pat so it adheres to the meat.

Build a charcoal and/or wood fire on one side of the grill, leaving the other side void. This will create two zones for cooking, indirect and direct. Grill the tri-tip directly over the hot coals (approximately 500°F) for 4 to 5 minutes on each side. Move the beef to the cool side of the grill (approximately 300°F), close the cover, and cook for an additional 30 minutes, or until the internal temperature of the tri-tip reaches 135 to 145°F for medium-rare to medium.

Let the beef rest under tented foil for 15 minutes before slicing.

STANDING RIB ROAST
with Roasted Garlic Herb Butter

SERVES: 6 TO 9

COOKING METHOD:
INDIRECT HEAT

SUGGESTED WOOD:
HICKORY, OAK

**COOKING TIME: 45 MINUTES
(ROASTED GARLIC HERB BUTTER)
2 TO 3 HOURS (RIB ROAST)**

★　★　★　★　★

**ROASTED GARLIC HERB
BUTTER**

4 GARLIC CLOVES

¼ TEASPOON DRIED THYME

¼ TEASPOON DRIED ROSEMARY

¼ TEASPOON DRIED OREGANO

1 TABLESPOON EXTRA-VIRGIN OLIVE OIL

¼ CUP BUTTER, SOFTENED

2- TO 3-BONE RIB ROAST WITH BONES
(APPROXIMATELY 4 TO 5 POUNDS)

1½ TABLESPOONS KOSHER SALT

1½ TEASPOONS CRACKED BLACK PEPPER

★　★　★　★　★

This expensive cut of beef is a primal cut taken from the upper rib area. A whole rib roast consists of seven ribs and weighs close to fifteen pounds, which is enough beef to feed a party of twenty. More typically this cut is sold as three to four rib roasts or is cut down to single rib-eye steaks.

Rib roasts are labeled many different ways at the grocery store, including as "standing rib roast" or "prime rib." The term "prime" is used very loosely in this case and probably does not mean the meat has been graded "prime" by the USDA.

Prime rib roasts have always been popular because of their tenderness and rich beef flavor. Usually the simpler preparation the better for this cut of beef. Many of the popular marinades today compromise the great taste of this cut by masking the natural beef flavor. This recipe uses mild seasoning accents to heighten and not diminish the flavor of this tasty beef roast.

Build a fire (wood or a combination of charcoal and wood) for indirect cooking by situating the coals on only one side of the grill, leaving the other side void.

On a doubled square of aluminum foil, place the garlic cloves, thyme, rosemary, and oregano. Drizzle the olive oil over the ingredients. Wrap the foil tight and place over the void side of the grill. Cook the foil pouch for 45 minutes at 250°F.

Remove the pouch from the cooker and open the foil. After cooling slightly, squeeze the garlic cloves from the husks into a small bowl. Mash the garlic and cooked herbs together, forming a paste. Stir in the softened butter and mix well. Spoon the mixture onto a sheet of plastic wrap and roll it into a small log. Refrigerate until firm, about 30 minutes, or up to 2 weeks.

Cut small slits every ¾ inch onto the top (the opposite side from the bones) of the rib roast. Slice the chilled garlic herb butter into pats and insert one into each slit, using the entire amount of butter. Season the rib roast evenly with the salt and pepper.

Place the rib roast on the void side of the grill with the bone side down and cook over indirect heat for 2 to 3 hours, or until the internal temperature reaches 120 to 125°F for rare, 130 to 135°F for medium rare, or 140 to 145°F for medium. Let the roast rest under tented foil for 20 minutes and then slice between each bone into thick steaks.

Below: Small pockets are cut in the standing rib roast and filled with pats of garlic herb butter to ensure a rich flavor. *Opposite:* An internal thermometer is the best way to gauge the doneness of this large cut of beef: 120°F = rare, 130°F = medium rare, 140°F = medium, 150°F = medium well, and 160°F = well done.

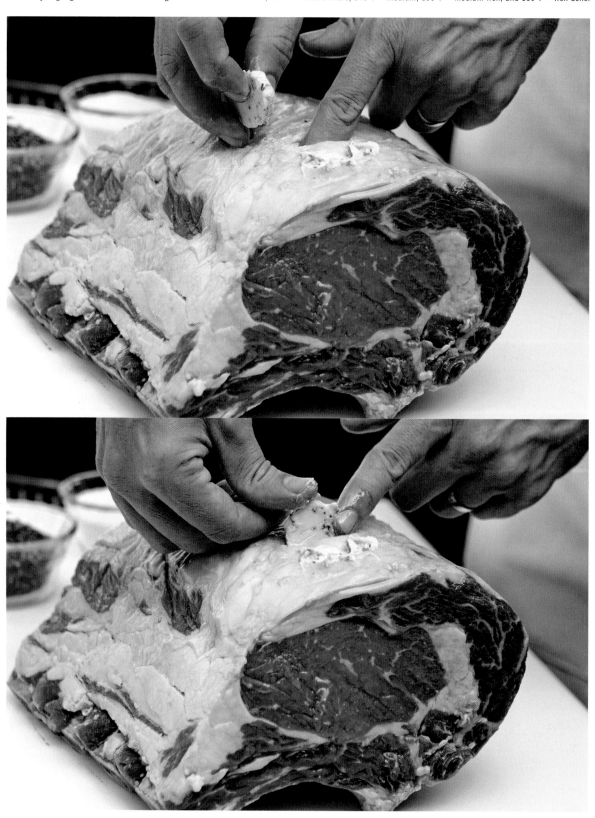

MUSHROOM-CRUSTED BEEF TENDERLOIN

SERVES: 10 TO 12

COOKING METHOD:
INDIRECT HEAT

SUGGESTED WOOD:
HICKORY, OAK, PECAN

COOKING TIME: 1 HOUR

★ ★ ★ ★ ★

MUSHROOM CRUST

5 TABLESPOONS BUTTER

1½ TABLESPOONS OLIVE OIL

3½ CUPS MINCED MUSHROOMS SUCH
AS BABY BELLA OR SHIITAKE

4 GARLIC CLOVES, MINCED

2 TABLESPOONS BALSAMIC VINEGAR

¾ TEASPOON DRIED OREGANO

1 TEASPOON SALT

1 WHOLE BEEF TENDERLOIN (APPROXIMATELY
6 POUNDS)

1½ TABLESPOONS KOSHER SALT

★ ★ ★ ★ ★

★ PITMASTER'S TIP ★

To ensure a more uniform doneness, let the meat
sit at room temperature for at least 30 minutes
before cooking.

The beef tenderloin is a major muscle that hangs between the shoulder blade and the hip under the rib cage. Because the tenderloin does very little work, it is the tenderest part of the cow. Weighing an average of six to eight pounds, the muscle is commonly cut into steak fillets, left whole, or cut into tenderloin roasts. No matter how it is prepared, it is considered a succulent deluxe cut, suitable for special occasions and celebrations.

Two things need to be done prior to cooking a whole tenderloin. First, the silver membrane, also called silver skin, that covers a portion of the outside of the tenderloin needs to be removed with a sharp knife. Second, to ensure even cooking, the thin tapered tail end of the tenderloin should be folded back on itself and tied with cooking twine to create a long roast of equal thickness throughout.

Although a very tender muscle, the tenderloin does not have the flavor depth of many other beef cuts. Too often people obscure its mild flavor with heavy rubs or marinades. Here a mushroom crust amplifies the flavor of the beef without compromising its natural flavors. With such a tender cut and the added flavor depth of the mushrooms, overcooking is the only way you can ruin this dish.

Melt the butter and oil together in a large skillet over medium heat. When the butter melts, add the minced mushrooms, garlic, balsamic vinegar, oregano, and salt. Simmer, stirring occasionally, for 4 minutes, or until the mushrooms start to soften. Remove from the heat and let cool.

Remove any silver membrane from the tenderloin with a sharp knife. Fold the tail of the tenderloin back onto itself and tie it with cooking twine (this creates a roast with a uniform thickness to ensure even doneness). Season the tenderloin with the kosher salt. Drain any excess liquid from the mushrooms. Pat the mushroom mixture evenly over all sides of the entire beef tenderloin, making a thin crust.

Build a fire (wood or a combination of charcoal and wood) for indirect cooking by situating the coals on only one side of the grill, leaving the other side void. When the cooker reaches 225°F, place the tenderloin on the void side of the grill and close the lid. Cook for 1 hour or until the internal temperature of the tenderloin reaches 120 to 125°F for rare, 130 to 135°F for medium rare, or 140 to 145°F for medium. Let the tenderloin rest under tented foil for at least 20 minutes before slicing.

BEEF KEBABS
with Mustard Horseradish Sauce

SERVES: 6

COOKING METHOD:
DIRECT HEAT

SUGGESTED SUPPLIES:
10-INCH BAMBOO SKEWERS,
SOAKED IN WATER

SUGGESTED WOOD: HICKORY,
OAK, MESQUITE

MARINATING TIME:
2 TO 6 HOURS

COOKING TIME:
8 TO 10 MINUTES

★   ★   ★   ★   ★

MARINADE

1 CUP SOY SAUCE

1 CUP VEGETABLE OIL

⅔ CUP BROWN SUGAR

6 TABLESPOONS GRANULATED SUGAR

¼ CUP APPLE CIDER VINEGAR

¼ CUP GROUND GINGER

¼ CUP GARLIC SALT

2 ONIONS

3 BELL PEPPERS

2½ POUNDS BEEF CHUNKS

MUSTARD HORSERADISH SAUCE (PAGE 229)

★   ★   ★   ★   ★

Traditionally barbecue involved cooking the toughest and largest cuts of meat—the cuts that nobody else wanted. Often when beef is butchered, scraps of meat are left piled on the cutting board. Some view this pile of discards as waste; others envision dinner. So it is with these beef skewers.

For this preparation you can use beef chunks left over from any of the cuts in this chapter: tenderloin tips, top round chunks, tri-tip scraps, and more. By adding vegetables to the skewer, you can stretch a small amount of beef to serve an entire family.

The marinade recipe figures prominently and fondly in my memories of the days before I joined the Big Bob Gibson family. When visiting my future in-laws Don McLemore (Big Bob's grandson) and his wife, Carolyn, I was treated to beef kebabs in this wonderfully balanced marinade. The sweet ginger and soy flavor is as good on veggies as it is on meat. I added the mustard horseradish sauce to take this recipe to the next level.

In a small bowl, combine the marinade ingredients and mix well. Cut the onions and peppers into 1-inch pieces. Divide the marinade between two bowls or two resealable plastic bags and add the meat to one and the vegetables to the other. Marinate in the refrigerator for 2 to 6 hours.

Remove the vegetables and meat from the marinade and discard any leftover liquid. Thread alternating pieces of onion, pepper, and meat onto the skewers.

Build a charcoal and/or wood fire for direct grilling. When the coals are hot (approximately 450 to 500°F), grill the kebabs directly over the coals for 8 to 10 minutes, turning once. When the meat starts to brown and firm, and the vegetables begin to char on the edges, remove the skewers from the grill. Serve with Mustard Horseradish Sauce.

GRILLED POTATO SALAD

SERVES: 4 TO 5

COOKING METHOD: DIRECT HEAT

COOKING TIME: 30 MINUTES

★ ★ ★ ★ ★

8 SLICES BACON

4 MEDIUM RED-SKIN POTATOES, DICED INTO ¾ INCH CUBES (5 CUPS)

1 LARGE WHITE ONION, CUT INTO THICK STRIPS

DRY RUB

2 TEASPOONS SALT

1¼ TEASPOONS BLACK PEPPER

1 TEASPOON PAPRIKA

1 TEASPOON GARLIC POWDER

¼ TEASPOON DRIED THYME

¼ TEASPOON DRIED ROSEMARY

⅛ TEASPOON CELERY SEED

DRESSING

5½ TABLESPOONS MAYONNAISE

2 TABLESPOONS DIJON MUSTARD

2 TEASPOONS WORCESTERSHIRE SAUCE

★ ★ ★ ★ ★

Sometimes it's good to buck tradition. This recipe breaks away from the creamy cold potato salad and tests the theory that "everything is better on the outdoor grill." This recipe, which I originally created for SOUTHERN LIVING magazine in 2009, answers the question with a resounding "Absolutely!"

Grilled Potato Salad starts with traditional ingredients such as potatoes, onions, mayonnaise, and mustard but takes an unfamiliar twist by utilizing a complex dry rub, which adds a vibrant punch of flavor. This unique recipe will draw raves served hot off the grill but is also good eatin' out of the fridge the next day.

In a large pan, fry the bacon. Remove the bacon from grease and set aside. Add the diced potatoes and onion to the bacon grease and stir until thoroughly coated. In a small bowl combine the dry rub ingredients and mix well. Add to the potatoes and onion and stir until coated.

Build a charcoal and/or wood fire for direct grilling. Pour the potatoes and onion into a slotted grill basket. Grill directly over the coals (approximately 450°F) on a covered grill for 30 minutes, stirring well every 5 minutes until the potatoes soften. Remove the potatoes and onion from the grill and place them into a medium-size bowl. Crumble the bacon and add it to the bowl.

In a small bowl combine the dressing ingredients and mix well. Pour the dressing over the potato and onion mixture and stir. Serve warm.

COAL-FIRED SWEET POTATOES

SERVES: 4
COOKING METHOD: COALS
COOKING TIME: 40 MINUTES

★ ★ ★ ★ ★

4 SWEET POTATOES, SKIN ON

MAPLE PECAN BUTTER
4 TABLESPOONS (½ STICK) BUTTER
¼ CUP PURE MAPLE SYRUP
3 TABLESPOONS CHOPPED PECANS
⅛ TEASPOON GROUND CINNAMON
⅛ TEASPOON CAYENNE PEPPER
⅛ TEASPOON SALT

★ ★ ★ ★ ★

The first time I made Coal-Fired Sweet Potatoes was at the Middleton Place plantation near Charleston, South Carolina, when Big Bob Gibson Bar-B-Q catered a food conference sponsored by Johnson & Wales University called "Cuisines of the Lowcountry and the Caribbean."

On the day of the dinner, every member of the Big Bob Gibson team was enlisted to do a cooking demonstration of the Caribbean fare. I am not sure whether my father-in-law, Don McLemore, drew the short straw or got the last pick, but somehow he was assigned the sweet potato ground pit. Imagine working at ground level in the dark over hot coals generating temperatures close to 1,000°F, all to cook an edible offering that looks like a smoldering meteorite. Under the sweat that dripped from his chin, Don wore a scowl all day—right up until dinner, when his sweet potatoes were the talk of the party. He was happy in the end, but I don't know if he'll ever let me live that one down.

For that event we served the potatoes with a Caribbean butter sauce, but here I suggest subbing a maple pecan butter. This is my favorite way to eat sweet potatoes, whether they are cooked in coals or baked in the oven. It is also a fantastic topping for sweet potato pancakes—but that is a different cookbook.

Place the sweet potatoes directly on a bed of hot coals. Cook for 40, minutes turning once halfway through.

Melt the butter in a small saucepan. Add the maple syrup, pecans, cinnamon, cayenne pepper, and salt. Heat the mixture on low for less than a minute, just until a layer of bubbles forms over the surface. Remove from the heat, but keep warm.

Remove the potatoes from the coals and brush away excess char. Split the potatoes lengthwise and top with the maple pecan butter.

Overleaf: Sweet potatoes roasting in a bed of hot coals.

STUFFED RED BELL PEPPERS
with Brown Sugar and Maple Baked Beans

SERVES: 8

**COOKING METHOD:
INDIRECT HEAT**

COOKING TIME: 50 MINUTES

★ ★ ★ ★ ★

1 LARGE ONION, CHOPPED

5 STRIPS BACON, CHOPPED

2 GARLIC CLOVES, CHOPPED

3 15-OUNCE CANS PINTO BEANS, DRAINED

3 15-OUNCE CANS KIDNEY BEANS, DRAINED

½ CUP BROWN SUGAR

½ CUP PURE MAPLE SYRUP

½ CUP BARBECUE SAUCE

¼ CUP KETCHUP

¼ CUP WORCESTERSHIRE SAUCE

1 TABLESPOON YELLOW MUSTARD

8 RED BELL PEPPERS

★ ★ ★ ★ ★

Few true barbecue recipes provide instant gratification, because time is the key element in producing magnificent results when cooking a whole beef brisket or pork shoulder. Baked bean recipes are similar in this regard. It takes time for all of the flavors to meld together to produce the perfect batch of beans.

While these peppers cook on the grill, the brown sugar and maple syrup caramelize to form a crust on top of the beans. The pepper makes a perfect cooking dish and serving bowl, while adding flavor to the slow-cooked beans.

Build a fire (wood or a combination of charcoal and wood) for indirect cooking by situating the coals on only one side of the grill, leaving the other side void. Preheat the cooker to 400°F.

In a small frying pan, sauté the onion and bacon together for 5 to 7 minutes, until the bacon starts to brown. Add the garlic and sauté for an additional 30 seconds. Drain the rendered bacon grease and scrape the mixture into a large bowl. Add the beans, brown sugar, maple syrup, barbecue sauce, ketchup, Worcestershire, and yellow mustard and mix well.

With a paring knife, slice off the top of each bell pepper. Pull out the core, veins, and seeds and discard. Fill each pepper with ¾ cup of the baked bean mix.

Place the peppers on the void side of the grill, close the lid and cook over indirect heat for 50 minutes, or until the filling is hot and crusty and the peppers soften.

GRILLED MARINATED MUSHROOMS

SERVES: 6

COOKING METHOD:
DIRECT HEAT

SUGGESTED SUPPLIES:
SOAKED WOODEN SKEWERS

COOKING TIME:
6 TO 10 MINUTES

★   ★   ★   ★   ★

MARINADE

1½ CUPS (3 STICKS) BUTTER

9 TABLESPOONS SOY MARINADE (PAGE 237)

3 TABLESPOONS OLIVE OIL

2½ TABLESPOONS BALSAMIC VINEGAR

¾ TEASPOON BLACK PEPPER

¾ TEASPOON DRIED OREGANO

1 POUND MUSHROOMS, ANY VARIETY

★   ★   ★   ★   ★

Legend has it that mushrooms are the key to immortality. They have been said to stimulate and sharpen our senses, and feats of superhuman strength have been attributed to them. Early Egyptians considered mushrooms to be food for royalty, barring their consumption by the commoners. Here in Alabama we suspect the pharaohs were partaking of the psychedelic variety. We do agree with one thing, though: Those little suckers are good eatin'.

There are very few foods that pair with beef as well as mushrooms do. Their savory and earthy flavors complement everything from steak and salads to satays. A marinade of soy, balsamic vinegar, and butter amplifies their natural gifts, while they caramelize on the grill. Serve these grilled delights with any recipe in this chapter. Also try topping them with Mustard Horseradish Sauce (page 229).

Melt the butter in a small saucepan. Add the remaining marinade ingredients, mix well, and heat just until warm. Pour the warm marinade over the mushrooms, stir to coat, and set aside at room temperature for 1 hour.

Build a charcoal and/or wood fire for direct grilling to 400°F. Thread the mushrooms onto skewers or place them in a grill basket and grill directly over the coals for 3 to 5 minutes on each side, basting frequently with the marinade.

PEACH BREAD PUDDING
with Vanilla-Peach Sauce

SERVES: 8

COOKING TIME: 1 HOUR

★ ★ ★ ★ ★

3 CUPS THICK-CUT WHITE BREAD, CRUST REMOVED, CUT INTO ¾-INCH CUBES

1½ CUPS WHOLE MILK

½ CUP HEAVY CREAM

4 TABLESPOONS (½ STICK) BUTTER

3 EGGS

½ CUP SUGAR

¾ TEASPOON VANILLA EXTRACT

2 TEASPOONS ALL-PURPOSE FLOUR

½ TEASPOON GROUND CINNAMON

1 CUP CHOPPED FRESH PEELED PEACHES

VANILLA-PEACH SAUCE

1 CUP HEAVY CREAM

¼ CUP SUGAR

¼ CUP PEACH NECTAR

1½ TEASPOONS CORNSTARCH

1 TABLESPOON WATER

1 TEASPOON PURE VANILLA EXTRACT

⅛ TEASPOON SALT

★ ★ ★ ★ ★

Like barbecue, bread pudding is a dessert with humble beginnings. The dish began as a way to recycle stale leftover bread into a simple filling and dessert through the addition of water and sugar.

Today, bread pudding is served at the finest white-tablecloth restaurants, and it is often made with specialty breads and fresh fruit. Instead of water, chefs substitute milk, cream, eggs, vanilla, and spices to create a creamy custard. To make this dessert more decadent, a ladle of rich and creamy sauce flavored with whiskey, rum, or vanilla is poured over the bread pudding.

Preheat the oven to 350°F. Place the bread cubes on a rimmed sheet pan and bake for 5 minutes, or until toasted to a light golden color. Remove the toasted cubes from the oven and place in the bottom of a 2-quart casserole dish.

In a medium saucepan, combine the milk, heavy cream, and butter. Warm over low heat until the butter melts; set aside.

In a medium bowl, whisk together the eggs, sugar, vanilla, flour, and cinnamon and beat well. With a wooden spoon, stir in the chopped peaches and the warm milk mixture. Pour the custard over the toasted bread cubes. Bake for 55 minutes, or until the center of the casserole is firm.

To make the vanilla-peach sauce, combine the cream, sugar, and peach nectar in a small saucepan and bring to a boil. Whisk the cornstarch with the water together in a small bowl, then stir into the boiling liquid. Reduce the heat and simmer for 1 minute, then stir in the vanilla and salt. Remove from the heat.

Cut the warm bread pudding into individual portions and top with warm vanilla-peach sauce.

CHAPTER 4

PIT-
FIRED
POUL-
TRY

★ ★ ★ ★ ★

When Big Bob Gibson was barbecuing, in the mid 1920s, the chicken farming industry was in its infancy. Like many farms of that era, the Gibson homestead raised livestock as well as poultry, both to produce income and to supply food for the family. In the nineteenth and early twentieth centuries, however, it was not the meat that made raising chickens on family farms lucrative, but their eggs. Eggs provided sustenance and could also be traded in local towns for other staple items. Whatever meager surplus of young males and old hens the farm produced was reserved for special-occasion meals. The chickens that made it to market were therefore expensive because the supply was very low. However, Bob was always able to ensure a supply of chicken to his restaurant thanks to his contacts with local farmers, and it has long been a fixture on his menus.

Today the chickens served at Big Bob Gibson Bar-B-Q weigh more than three pounds each, but in the early years sizing was irregular. The weight of whole chickens would fluctuate by as much as one pound, and Big Bob never knew what size chickens would be delivered to his back door. One thing he could control was which customers got the larger chickens. His friends or a young lady who caught his eye always left the restaurant with a heavy bag and a big smile. You could tell a lot from the size of a person's chicken!

★ ★ ★ ★ ★

There is much debate as to what is the best way to cook chickens. First, you must decide whether to keep it whole or cut it into pieces before cooking. Second, do you use a marinade, brine, dry rub, sauce, or some combination of flavorings? Is it best to cook the chicken hot and fast or low and slow? Last, there are the pitfalls specific to cooking chickens: dry breasts, rubbery skin, and little flavor.

At our restaurant, the problems associated with cooking chickens have been addressed the Big Bob Gibson way. First, "keep it whole." Larger cuts of chicken hold more juices longer. Second, "keep it simple." Too many flavorings overpower the taste of the chicken. Next, "keep it moist." An oil baste ensures juicy meat. Finally, "cook with indirect heat." A hot fire coupled with indirect cooking results in chicken skin that is thin, crisp, and tasty.

One drawback to leaving a chicken whole is an uneven cook. Whole chickens are shaped like a football, and they require attention and rotation. A flat grill will accentuate the problem by cooking the side closest to the fire at a higher rate. Getting around this problem can be as simple as making one cut down the backbone of the chicken, which allows the chicken to be opened up flat, turning an oval problem into a two-sided answer.

A whole chicken is made up of both white and dark meats. The white meat is very lean, while the dark meat has a higher fat content, which means they will not reach optimum doneness at the same time. The lean breast meat starts to decline in moisture when the internal temperature passes 160°F. The thigh and leg pieces will fare well up to an internal temperature of 180°F. This means that often the breast has passed perfection by the time the dark meat is finally done. Positioning the chicken strategically on the grill, where the dark meat acts as a buffer between the fire and the white meat, is the solution to this common problem.

There are a couple of advantages to consider when debating whether to cut the chicken prior to cooking. Although cutting the chicken means less protection for the meat, it also gives you more control in reaching optimum doneness. You no longer have to worry about juggling the internal temperatures of white and dark meat if you separate the two. Second, slicing whole chickens into pieces gives the marinade, dry rub, or brine better access to the meat, resulting in more flavorful fowl.

In this chapter, we explore a multitude of chicken cuts and different cooking methods as well. Some of the same logic used for cooking chickens can be applied to both of this chapter's turkey dishes. Of course, all of the recipes, both old and new, begin with the techniques preached by Big Bob Gibson since 1925.

"WE WORKED THREE DAYS AND THREE NIGHTS AND DIDN'T EVEN PULL OUR SHOES OFF."

DUTCH DRAKE

1950s

In 1950, Bob Gibson's latest restaurant had grown from a four-table barbecue stand to a highly successful twenty-five–table eating establishment. **Big Bob Gibson Bar-B-Q remained a popular gathering spot for locals but also gained a reputation as a prime meeting place for travelers and businessmen, establishing the restaurant as a Decatur landmark.**

Big Bob Gibson's new drive for business led to booking off-site catering events. Parties for the American Legion with 500 pounds of pork and for Monsanto with barbecue chicken for 1,800 people were commonplace. This would have been great if the restaurant had been able to handle the extra business, but often Big Bob overextended his thriving enterprise.

The first problem was labor. Big Bob Gibson Bar-B-Q was fully staffed in the front of the house with waitresses, but his pitroom help was slim. Big Bob, Dutch Drake, and a teenage upstart named Jerry "Red" Knighten "manned the shovels." Manning the shovels is exactly what they did. If the catering order was too large for their cooker to handle, they dug new pits in the back. During peak times, they used a 4 x 8-foot cooker indoors and three 4 x 40-foot pits outside. Holes were cut in the bottom of steel barrels and wood was burned until hot coals spilled from the openings. Long shovels were used to scatter the coals in the makeshift cookers. It was imperative to keep a long vigil over the fire.

The next hurdle was product supply. In those days, commercial distribution of pork, poultry, and beef was often unreliable. After committing to large parties, Bob Gibson often spent the afternoons scouring the countryside for more meat when his suppliers were unable to deliver enough quantity. Sometimes this meant butchering their own. In one case, prior to a Monsanto party, eighty live hogs and fifteen chicken pens were delivered to Big Bob's back door by a local farmer.

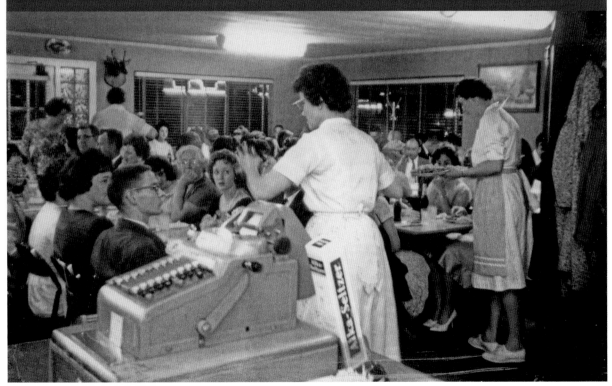

Waitresses manage a full house at Big Bob Gibson Bar-B-Q.

BIG BOB GIBSON'S BARBECUE – HIW

31, SO. – PH. 9296 – DECATUR, ALA.

In this postcard, you can see the neon pig wearing a chef's hat and the huge brick chimney that were focal points of the restaurant in the early 1950s.

BIG BOB GIBSON BAR-B-Q CHICKEN
with White Sauce

SERVES: 4 TO 8

COOKING METHOD:
INDIRECT HEAT

SUGGESTED WOOD:
HICKORY

COOKING TIME:
3 HOURS

★ ★ ★ ★ ★

2 WHOLE BUTTERFLIED CHICKENS

1 TABLESPOON SALT

½ CUP OIL (VEGETABLE, OLIVE, LARD)

2 TEASPOONS BLACK PEPPER

BIG BOB GIBSON BAR-B-Q WHITE SAUCE
(PAGE 218)

★ ★ ★ ★ ★

Q: I am a big fan of cooking whole chicken. Sometimes when I cook it it is perfectly moist, other times dry, and I have even served it raw in places. My problem comes when trying to decide when the chicken is done. Help me!

A: Remember that the last part on the whole chicken to finish cooking is always the joint between the leg and the thigh. The easiest way to tell if your chicken is perfect is a simple twist test. Twist a chicken leg with your fingers. If it doesn't budge, it isn't done. If it spins like a roulette wheel in Las Vegas, it has cooked too long. Ideally you want to feel slight tension and then a release of the joint.

This is one of the most popular menu items at Big Bob Gibson Bar-B-Q and has been a staple in Decatur, Alabama, since Big Bob first started selling his 'Q in 1925. Most folks raised in North Alabama have firmly believed since childhood that barbecue sauce is white. Where did the rest of the country go wrong?

The simple technique for cooking the chickens has not changed for more than eighty years, and the ingredients can be listed on one hand: salt, pepper, basting oil, and, of course, that creamy, tangy, peppery white sauce. An all-hickory fire on a closed brick pit is the only other necessity for duplicating the authentic Big Bob flavors.

The type of oil used for basting has changed through the years. Big Bob used whatever oil was most easily available to baste the chickens as they cooked, including rendered lard. Excess fat was cut off the pork shoulders and heated in a pot until the lard liquefied. The rendered lard was stored in metal "lard buckets" until needed. No matter what type of oil is used, the chickens still taste fantastic.

Build a fire (wood or a combination of charcoal and wood) for indirect cooking by situating the coals on only one side of the cooker, leaving the other side void. Preheat the cooker to 325°F.

Dust each whole chicken evenly with salt. Place the chickens over the void side of the cooker, with the skin side up. When the skin on the chicken is golden brown, after about 1½ hours, turn the chickens skin side down, basting both sides with the oil. Sprinkle the cavities of each chicken evenly with pepper. Cook the chicken for an additional 1½ hours or until the internal temperature of the thickest part of the thigh reaches 180°F. Add more wood to the fire as needed to replenish the supply of coals and maintain a temperature of 325°F.

Pour the white sauce into a narrow, deep container and position it next to your cooker. Remove each chicken from the cooking grate and submerge it into the pot of white sauce. Remove the chicken from the sauce, cut each chicken in half between the breasts, and then quarter by cutting between each breast and thigh.

Below: Halfway through the cooking process, Big Bob Gibson's chickens are seasoned liberally with coarse ground black pepper. *Opposite:* Whole chickens are cooked fifty at a time in the pits at Big Bob Gibson Bar-B-Q.

★ PITMASTER'S TIP ★

When cooking whole chickens over indirect heat, point the legs toward the fire. This will ensure that the leaner breast meat will not be overdone before the dark meat is fully cooked.

"AT TIMES THERE WERE MORE FEATHERS THAN FIREWOOD BEHIND THE RESTAURANT."

JERRY KNIGHTEN

LOAF-PAN CHICKEN

SERVES: 4

COOKING METHOD:
INDIRECT HEAT

SUGGESTED WOOD:
HICKORY, APPLE, APRICOT

COOKING TIME:
2 TO 2½ HOURS

★ ★ ★ ★ ★

¾ CUP APPLESAUCE

3 TABLESPOONS WORCESTERSHIRE SAUCE

1 WHOLE CHICKEN (3½ POUNDS)

DRY RUB

1 TABLESPOON TURBINADO SUGAR

2¼ TEASPOONS PAPRIKA

1½ TEASPOONS BLACK PEPPER

1½ TEASPOONS GARLIC SALT

¾ TEASPOON CELERY SALT

¾ TEASPOON SALT

¼ TEASPOON GROUND CUMIN

¼ TEASPOON GROUND CORIANDER

★ ★ ★ ★ ★

Have you ever tried a beer-can chicken recipe? That's when a whole chicken is perched atop a beer can and set on the grill, so the beer steams from the can and keeps the sitting bird from drying out. The results are tender and moist, but sometimes the flavor is washed out; and if the chicken falls over it can be a mess.

Loaf-Pan Chicken is a dummy-proof alternative to beer-can chicken, although the technique is not as gimmicky. You simply set the bird in a loaf pan and place it, pan and all, on the grill. The loaf pan captures all the juices and increases the humidity surrounding the chicken. The result is tender and moist meat every time, and best of all, the flavor is full and undiluted.

Build a fire (wood or a combination of charcoal and wood) for indirect cooking by situating the coals on only one side of the cooker, leaving the other side void.

In a small bowl, stir together the applesauce and Worcestershire. Holding the chicken over a 9 x 5 x 3-inch loaf pan, pour the mixture over the chicken, making sure the chicken is thoroughly coated both inside and out. Let the excess liquid drip into the loaf pan.

In another small bowl, combine the dry rub ingredients and mix well. Coat the entire chicken, both inside and out, with the dry rub. Place the chicken into the loaf pan, breast side up.

When the grill temperature reaches approximately 300°F, place the loaf pan on the grill grate away from the coals, close the cover, and cook for 2 hours, or until the internal temperature of the chicken thigh reaches 175°F. Let the chicken cool a bit in the pan before cutting into serving pieces.

AIRLINE CHICKEN BREAST
with Basil Butter

SERVES: 4

COOKING METHOD:
DIRECT AND INDIRECT HEAT

SUGGESTED WOOD:
HICKORY, PECAN, OAK

COOKING TIME: 40 MINUTES

★ ★ ★ ★ ★

4 CHICKEN BREASTS (SKIN-ON BREAST WITH
ONLY THE WING DRUMETTE ATTACHED)

KOSHER SALT

BLACK PEPPER

BASIL BUTTER

12 TABLESPOONS (1½ STICKS) BUTTER

½ CUP CHOPPED FRESH BASIL

★ ★ ★ ★ ★

★ PITMASTER'S TIP ★
The more times chickens are cut, the more natural moisture is lost during the cooking process. More pieces means less juice.

For years Big Bob Gibson Bar-B-Q customers have wondered why their chicken breasts were sometimes served without a portion of the wing. Usually it's because at some point during the process of flipping, basting, and moving the whole chickens around, the wing tips get caught in the cooking grate and break off. That being said, Big Bob **loved** chicken wings.

While a skin-on chicken breast with only the drumette of the wing attached was called a "taster" in the early days of the restaurant, in the 1960s, back when commercial airlines still served real meals, they became known as "airline chicken." Leaving a portion of the wing attached to a small chicken breast made the serving look larger while still allowing it to fit nicely into an airline food tray.

The airline chicken breast is a perfect cut for the outdoor grill if cooked correctly. The best method is a combination of both direct and indirect cooking. With a portion of the wing removed, the skin covering the breast is exposed so it can become thin and crispy while acting as a protective barrier to the lean meat. Finishing the chicken in a pan over indirect heat protects the exposed breast meat.

With a sharp knife, remove the bones and cartilage from the underside of each chicken breast. The only bone left in the breasts should be the drumette bone. Season the chicken breasts lightly on both sides with salt and black pepper.

Build a charcoal and/or wood fire on one side of the grill, leaving the other side void. This will create two cooking zones, indirect and direct. The heat over the coals should be very hot (approximately 450 to 500°F).

Melt the butter in a small pan. Add the basil and mix well. Place the chicken breasts directly over the coals skin side down and baste with half the basil butter. Grill the chicken for 5 minutes, or until the skin is golden brown and crisp. Transfer the chicken to a shallow baking pan skin side up and place it over the void side of the grill. Baste with the remaining basil butter. Cover the grill and cook with indirect heat (approximately 400°F) for an additional 35 minutes. The internal temperature of the chicken breasts should reach 160°F. Slice the chicken breasts across the skin into small medallions to serve.

GRILLED CHICKEN AND TOMATO SALAD
with Balsamic Vinaigrette

SERVES: 4

COOKING METHOD:
DIRECT AND INDIRECT HEAT

SUGGESTED WOOD:
HICKORY, PECAN, OAK

MARINATING TIME:
4 TO 12 HOURS

COOKING TIME: **10 MINUTES**

* * * * *

MARINADE

1 CUP EXTRA-VIRGIN OLIVE OIL

¾ CUP WORCESTERSHIRE SAUCE

¼ CUP SOY SAUCE

1 TABLESPOON FRESH LEMON JUICE

2 TEASPOONS MINCED GARLIC

1¾ TEASPOONS SALT

1 TEASPOON GROUND WHITE PEPPER

4 BONELESS SKINLESS CHICKEN BREASTS

3 PLUM TOMATOES

1 YELLOW TOMATO

⅓ CUP DICED SWEET ONIONS, SUCH AS VIDALIA

1 TABLESPOON COARSELY CHOPPED FRESH BASIL

DRESSING

1½ TABLESPOONS EXTRA-VIRGIN OLIVE OIL

1½ TEASPOONS BALSAMIC VINEGAR

½ TEASPOON CIDER VINEGAR

SALT AND BLACK PEPPER

4 THICK SLICES MOZZARELLA CHEESE

* * * * *

A flourishing garden filled with home-grown vegetables was a source of pride to Big Bob, and his favorite area of the garden was the tomato patch, where he tended a variety of cultivars. By planting different kinds of tomato plants, he was ensured fresh ripe tomatoes all summer long. His favorite summer dish was a tomato salad made with whatever types of tomatoes were in season.

This recipe combines two of Big Bob's Southern favorites: grilled chicken and tomato salad. It is hard to beat the sweet taste of tomatoes in season combined with the charred flavors of chicken cooked outdoors. Each element of this dish can be served on its own, but together they form a signature dish that you'll return to again and again all summer long.

Combine the marinade ingredients in a shallow baking dish or a resealable plastic bag. Add the chicken breasts, turn to coat, and cover or seal the bag. Marinate the chicken in the refrigerator for at least 4 hours and up to 12 hours.

Dice the plum and yellow tomatoes into medium-size chunks and place in a small mixing bowl. Add the diced onions and basil to the mixture and set aside. Combine the dressing ingredients in a small bowl, pour over the tomato mixture, and toss lightly; season with salt and pepper to taste and toss again. The tomato salad can be served at room temperature or refrigerated until ready to use.

Build a charcoal and/or wood fire on one side of grill, leaving the other side void. This will create two zones for cooking, indirect and direct. Heat the grill to approximately 400°F. Remove the chicken breasts from the marinade and place on the grill, directly over the heat. Grill for 5 to 6 minutes on each side, or until golden brown and firm to the touch. The internal temperature of the chicken breasts should be 160°F.

Move the chicken breasts away from the fire and place a thick slice of mozzarella cheese on each one. Close the lid and cook until the cheese starts to soften, about 1 minute.

To serve, top the grilled chicken with a generous amount of tomato salad.

BRINED CHICKEN
with White Sauce

SERVES: 8

COOKING METHOD:
DIRECT HEAT

SUGGESTED WOOD:
HICKORY, PECAN, OAK

BRINING TIME: 1 HOUR

COOKING TIME: 12 MINUTES

★ ★ ★ ★ ★

BRINE

1 CUP APPLE JUICE

1 CUP WATER

1 TABLESPOON SALT

¼ TABLESPOON GARLIC POWDER

1 TABLESPOON HONEY

½ TABLESPOON DARK BROWN SUGAR

½ TABLESPOON SOY SAUCE

½ TABLESPOON FRESH LEMON JUICE

8 BONELESS SKINLESS CHICKEN BREASTS

BIG BOB GIBSON BAR-B-Q WHITE SAUCE
(PAGE 218)

★ ★ ★ ★ ★

A brine is a great way to ensure a moist and juicy chicken—or any other type of meat. Brines are simply liquid marinades with a high salt content. All meat contains salt, and when it is submerged in a liquid with a higher salt content, the liquid is absorbed into the meat through a process called osmosis. The meat retains the moisture, helping to yield juicy results on the grill.

The following sweet brine recipe works well on skinless chicken breasts. The liquid brine not only prevents the chicken from drying out but provides extra flavor. When the meat is combined with the tangy white sauce, it makes a fantastic addition to salads and quesadillas, and it tastes great on its own as an entrée.

In a medium bowl, combine the brine ingredients and mix well. Add the chicken breasts, making sure they are completely covered. Cover the bowl and refrigerate for 1 hour. Remove the chicken breasts from the brine and wipe off the excess salt.

Preheat an outdoor grill to 400°F. Place the chicken breasts on the grate directly over the heat and grill for 5 to 6 minutes on each side, or until golden brown and firm to the touch. The internal temperature of the chicken breasts should be 160°F.

Submerge each chicken breast into a bowl of Big Bob Gibson Bar-B-Q White Sauce. Remove from the sauce and serve.

★ **PITMASTER'S TIP** ★

The natural shape of the chicken breast is thick on one end and very thin on the other. To even out the thickness, press firmly with the heel of your hand on the thickest part of each breast immediately prior to putting it on the grill. This will ensure more even cooking.

BARBECUE CHICKEN BREASTS
with Soy-Lemon Marinade

MAKES: 6 SERVINGS

COOKING METHOD:
INDIRECT HEAT

SUGGESTED WOOD:
HICKORY, OAK

MARINATING TIME:
30 TO 45 MINUTES

COOKING TIME: 16 MINUTES

★ ★ ★ ★ ★

SOY-LEMON MARINADE

8 TABLESPOONS (1 STICK) BUTTER

1 CUP SOY SAUCE

½ CUP FRESH LEMON JUICE

1½ TEASPOONS BLACK PEPPER

1¼ TEASPOONS GARLIC POWDER

1¼ TEASPOONS ONION POWDER

1¼ TEASPOONS GROUND GINGER

1¼ TEASPOONS PAPRIKA

1¼ TEASPOONS SUGAR

1¼ TEASPOONS MSG (OPTIONAL)

6 BONELESS AND SKINLESS CHICKEN BREASTS

★ ★ ★ ★ ★

Lemons have a broad appeal for those who barbecue because of the variety of ways in which they can be used. Lemon slices heighten both the color and flavor of sop mops or bastes and sauces, and a sprinkling of lemon on fresh-cut fruits will prevent oxidation, which causes fruits to turn brown before they can hit the grill. A twist of lemon will neutralize the odor of fish, a must for cedar plank–smoked salmon. Perhaps most important, in a marinade the acid in lemon juice will help break down the meat's collagen fibers, thus helping to tenderize tougher cuts.

This recipe, cooked using the indirect heat method at high temperature, is easily one of the quickest and most flavorful recipes I know. Cooking with indirect heat at a high temperature on a closed grill will simulate an indoor oven without sacrificing smoke flavor and will prevent premature caramelization of the soy sauce.

Melt the butter in a small saucepan. Remove from the heat and add the remaining marinade ingredients. Mix until well blended. Place the chicken in a shallow dish or a resealable plastic bag. Reserve 1 cup of the marinade for basting, and then pour the remaining marinade over the chicken. Cover the dish or seal the bag and marinate the chicken in the refrigerator for 30 to 45 minutes.

Build a fire (wood or a combination of charcoal and wood) for indirect cooking by situating the coals on only one side of the cooker, leaving the other side void. When the temperature reaches 400°F, remove the chicken from the marinade and place it on the grill grate, away from the coals. Cook covered for 8 minutes, then flip the chicken and baste with the reserved marinade. Cook the chicken for 8 minutes longer, or until the internal temperature reaches 160°F.

★ PITMASTER'S TIP ★

A room-temperature lemon will juice much more easily than a lemon straight out of the refrigerator. When making recipes such as Soy-Lemon Marinade, three tablespoons of juice per lemon can be expected. To get even more juice from your lemon, roll it along a work surface, pressing firmly, before slicing and squeezing.

SMOKED LEG QUARTERS
with Fresh Herbs

SERVES: 4 TO 6

COOKING METHOD:
INDIRECT HEAT

SUGGESTED WOOD:
HICKORY, OAK

MARINATING TIME:
8 TO 10 HOURS

COOKING TIME:
1 HOUR 30 MINUTES

★ ★ ★ ★ ★

MARINADE

1 CUP EXTRA-VIRGIN OLIVE OIL

½ CUP FRESH LEMON JUICE

1 TABLESPOON MINCED GARLIC

1¾ TEASPOONS KOSHER SALT

1 TEASPOON BLACK PEPPER

¾ TEASPOON CAYENNE PEPPER

6 TABLESPOONS CHOPPED FRESH FLAT-LEAF
PARSLEY LEAVES

2 TABLESPOONS CHOPPED FRESH BASIL LEAVES

2 TABLESPOONS CHOPPED FRESH OREGANO
LEAVES

2 TABLESPOONS CHOPPED FRESH CILANTRO
LEAVES

6 CHICKEN LEG-THIGH QUARTERS

★ ★ ★ ★ ★

Nine times out of ten when chicken is ordered in a restaurant, a breast will arrive at the table. Where is the love for dark meat? To my mind there is no comparison between the depth of flavors of dark meat versus white meat. On top of that, chicken legs and thighs stay moister and more tender and have a greater margin of error when cooking. For those reasons most competitive barbecuers prefer to submit dark meat rather than chicken breast to trained judges.

For marinating chicken it is hard to beat a traditional Italian dressing. The marinade in this recipe stays close to this philosophy while adding a fresh punch with mixed herbs. Its earthy acidic profile complements the subtle smoke flavor of the chicken; there is nothing out-of-the-bottle about it.

Mix the marinade ingredients in a small bowl and whisk until well blended. Reserve ½ cup of marinade for basting and then pour the remainder into a shallow dish or a resealable plastic bag. Add the chicken and turn to coat. Cover the dish or seal the bag and marinate the chicken in the refrigerator for 8 to 12 hours.

Build a fire (wood or a combination of charcoal and wood) for indirect cooking. When the temperature is approximately 300°F, remove the chicken from the marinade and place on the grill, skin side up, away from the coals. Cook for 45 minutes, then flip the chicken, baste with the reserved marinade, and cook for an additional 45 minutes, or until the internal temperature reaches 175°F.

★ PITMASTER'S TIP ★

A plastic sealable freezer bag is your best option for marinating foods. These bags are nonreactive and mess free. Place the food and marinade into the bag, press to remove air, and seal tight. Place the bag into a bowl or on a rimmed plate just in case of leaks and put it in the refrigerator. No flipping and turning are required. Better yet, there is no cleanup.

SPICY APRICOT WINGS

SERVES: 4 TO 6

COOKING METHOD:
INDIRECT HEAT

SUGGESTED WOOD:
HICKORY, APRICOT, APPLE

MARINATING TIME:
4 HOURS

COOKING TIME:
30 TO 35 MINUTES

★   ★   ★   ★   ★

MARINADE

1 CUP APRICOT PRESERVES

¼ CUP WORCESTERSHIRE SAUCE

¼ CUP BROWN SUGAR

2 TABLESPOONS SOY SAUCE

2 TABLESPOONS DIJON MUSTARD

2 TABLESPOONS KOSHER SALT

4 TEASPOONS BLACK PEPPER

2 TEASPOONS GARLIC POWDER

2 TEASPOONS PAPRIKA

1 TEASPOON CAYENNE PEPPER

½ TEASPOON GROUND GINGER

14 WHOLE CHICKEN WINGS CUT INTO
WINGS AND DRUMETTES (28 PIECES TOTAL;
SEE PITMASTER'S TIP, PAGE 134)

★   ★   ★   ★   ★

If there is one fruit whose flavor melds perfectly with chicken, it is the apricot, but incorporating juice or fruit chunks into barbecue sauce can give grilled foods a charred fruit flavor. The alternative is a fruity marinade that can be tasted throughout the meat, not just on the skin. The recipe gives fruit lovers (and wing lovers) the best of both worlds in one simple step, as the marinade forms a sweet glaze while the chicken cooks.

Mix the marinade ingredients in a small bowl and whisk until well blended. Place the chicken in a shallow dish or resealable plastic bag and pour the marinade over the wings, turning to coat. Cover or seal, and marinate the wings in the refrigerator for 4 hours.

Build a charcoal and/or wood fire on one side of the grill, leaving the other side void. This will create an area for indirect heat. When the temperature reaches 450°F, remove the wings from the marinade (do not shake off the excess marinade) and place them on the grill grate away from the coals. Close the lid and cook for approximately 30 to 35 minutes, flipping each wing piece once. Remove the wings from the grill and serve.

PEPPERED WINGS
with Caramelized Soy and Blackberry Glaze

SERVES: 4 TO 6

COOKING METHOD:
INDIRECT HEAT

SUGGESTED WOOD:
HICKORY, CHERRY, PECAN

COOKING TIME: 30 MINUTES

★ ★ ★ ★ ★

DRY RUB

2 TEASPOONS SALT

2 TEASPOONS BROWN SUGAR

2 TEASPOONS BLACK PEPPER

1 TEASPOON PAPRIKA

⅛ TEASPOON CAYENNE PEPPER

⅛ TEASPOON WHITE PEPPER

14 WHOLE CHICKEN WINGS, CUT INTO WINGS AND DRUMETTES (28 PIECES TOTAL; SEE PITMASTER'S TIP, BELOW)

CARAMELIZED SOY AND BLACKBERRY GLAZE
(PAGE 230)

★ ★ ★ ★ ★

For a snack before, during, or after the ball game there is no better food than the chicken wing. The great thing about chicken wings is their versatility. Spicy, sweet, salty, sticky, saucy, or dry are all options when cooking wings on the grill. I generally prefer my chicken wings seasoned with a dry rub and grilled; in my opinion, sauce tends to cover up the crispy, salty-peppery flavor of dry wings. With that said, however, I do love this recipe. The glaze adds flavor that goes way beyond what you would expect from a grilled wing. For those who like a sticky molasses flavor with a fruity edge, you've just found your new favorite wing recipe.

Stir together the dry rub ingredients in a small bowl. Season the wings with all of the rub for extra-hot wings or half of the rub for spicy.

Build a charcoal and/or wood fire on one side of the grill, leaving the other side void. This will create an area for indirect cooking away from the coals. When the cooker temperature reaches 450°F, place the wings on the grill grate away from the coals and close the cooker lid. Cook for approximately 30 minutes, flipping each wing once.

When the wings are brown and crisp, remove them from the grill and drizzle with warm Caramelized Soy and Blackberry Glaze.

★ PITMASTER'S TIP ★

A whole chicken wing is shaped like the letter *Z* and comprised of three parts: the drumette, the wing, and the wing tip. Before grilling, cut the joints separating the three parts with a sharp knife or poultry shears. Discard the bony wing tips, and the remaining two parts are ready to go.

SMOKED THANKSGIVING TURKEY

SERVES: 8 TO 10

**COOKING METHOD:
INDIRECT HEAT**

**SUGGESTED WOOD:
HICKORY, OAK**

COOKING TIME: 6 HOURS

★ ★ ★ ★ ★

1 12- TO 14-POUND WHOLE TURKEY,
FRESH OR THAWED

2 TEASPOONS SALT

1 TEASPOON BLACK PEPPER

1 CUP (2 STICKS) BUTTER, SOFTENED

★ ★ ★ ★ ★

Q: I have all but stopped cooking whole turkeys for Thanksgiving because it is too much meat. When I cook a skinless turkey breast, my family devours the white meat despite the dry shell that forms on the outside. What can I do to solve the problem?

A: When the skin and bone are removed from a lean cut of meat such as a turkey breast, there is nothing left to protect the meat from drying out during the cooking process. Your best bet is to coat the breast with a liquid or paste with a high fat or oil content prior to seasoning. This will keep that dry shell from forming and make everyone in your family happy.

Sometimes, "simple" and "expected" trump "gourmet" and "unusual." There are many recipes floating around that try to dress up this annual dish. The results are flavors that are foreign to both the meat and the occasion.

The most unique thing about this recipe is the technique, which involves wrapping the bird in aluminum foil with a hole cut in the top. This step is beneficial in two ways: First, it helps to trap moisture and increases the humidity in the air around the turkey. Second, the hole in the foil allows in just enough true smoke to flavor the turkey so you don't run the risk of ruining your feast with the harsh bitter flavor of an over-smoked turkey.

Build a charcoal and/or wood fire on one side of the grill, leaving the other side void. This will create an area for indirect heat.

Place the turkey in an aluminum roasting pan, breast side up, and season it both inside and out with the salt and pepper. Using your hands, mold the softened butter into a ball about 2 inches in diameter. Press the ball firmly onto the top of the turkey breast. Cover the roasting pan with two sheets of heavy aluminum foil and seal tightly. With a knife, cut a 2 x 1-inch hole in the foil directly over the mound of butter.

It is very important that the butter on top of the breast be mounded about 2 inches high. This will create a steam cavity between the aluminum foil and the turkey when the butter melts and will also give room for the smoke to circulate around the turkey.

When the temperature of the cooker reaches 250°F, place the turkey in its pan on the grill away from the heat. Cover the grill and cook the turkey for 6 hours, or until the internal temperature of the thickest part of the thigh reaches 170 to 175°F.

Note: Near the end of the cooking process look through the hole in the foil to determine how the turkey is browning. If the turkey looks white or pale, tear the foil open on top to increase smoke penetration and encourage the browning process.

SMOKED TURKEY BREAST
with Honey-Maple Glaze

SERVES: 6 TO 8

COOKING METHOD:
INDIRECT HEAT

SUGGESTED WOOD:
HICKORY, OAK, MAPLE

COOKING TIME: 3 HOURS

★ ★ ★ ★ ★

WET RUB

2 TEASPOONS BROWN MUSTARD

2 TEASPOONS EXTRA-VIRGIN OLIVE OIL

DRY RUB

1 TABLESPOON DARK BROWN SUGAR

1 TEASPOON GARLIC SALT

1 TEASPOON CELERY SALT

1 TEASPOON PAPRIKA

½ TEASPOON BLACK PEPPER

¼ TEASPOON CAYENNE PEPPER

1 BONELESS SKINLESS TURKEY BREAST,
ABOUT 4 POUNDS

HONEY-MAPLE GLAZE

4 TABLESPOONS (½ STICK) BUTTER

3 TABLESPOONS PURE MAPLE SYRUP

1 TABLESPOON HONEY

★ ★ ★ ★ ★

When a whole turkey is a little too much meat for your gathering, a turkey breast is a great option. The bad news is that most turkey breasts sold in grocery stores are seasoned, precooked, and in some cases processed. If raw turkey breasts are not a staple in your grocery-store meat case, ask your butcher for boneless turkey breast lobes.

The other way to obtain raw boneless breasts is to cut your own, which is a simple process. Beginning with a whole turkey, place your knife parallel to the backbone. Cut straight down about three inches following the backbone until your knife reaches the rib cage. Follow the rib cage with the knife, cutting away from the backbone. This will separate the breast lobe from the whole turkey. Repeat the process on the other side of the turkey to yield a second boneless turkey breast. Freeze the remaining turkey for future use.

Build a charcoal and/or wood fire on one side of the grill, leaving the other side void. This will create an area for indirect heat.

In separate small bowls, combine the wet rub and dry rub ingredients and mix well. Apply the wet rub to the entire turkey breast, coating it thoroughly, then sprinkle the dry rub over the turkey as well.

When the cooker reaches 250°F, place the turkey breast on the grill away from the heat and cook for 2½ hours. While it cooks, melt the butter in a small saucepan and stir in the maple syrup and honey. After 2½ hours, coat the turkey breast with half of the glaze; cook for an additional 15 minutes, and then coat the turkey with the remaining glaze. Cook for 15 minutes more, or until the internal temperature of the thickest part of the breast reaches 165°F.

Remove the turkey from the grill and let it rest under tented foil for 15 to 20 minutes before carving. Slice into medallions by cutting across the turkey breast.

MARINATED COLESLAW

SERVES: 8 TO 10

★ ★ ★ ★ ★

1 LARGE HEAD OF CABBAGE, SHREDDED

1 ONION, CHOPPED FINE

1 LARGE GREEN BELL PEPPER, CORED, SEEDED, AND CHOPPED FINE

1 CELERY STALK, CHOPPED FINE

1½ CUPS SUGAR

1 CUP CIDER VINEGAR

¾ CUP VEGETABLE OIL

1 TABLESPOON SALT

★ ★ ★ ★ ★

Coleslaw is a staple side dish in every barbecue restaurant in the South, and the flavors vary from region to region. You'll find hot slaw, mustard slaw, creamy slaw, vinegar slaw, red slaw, white slaw, and even blue cheese slaw. Which is better usually depends on the flavors you grew up with or what entrée you are serving it with, and although the debates aren't as heated as those focusing on politics or who has the best 'Q, the discussions are quite passionate.

This marinated coleslaw recipe is one of the stable of slaws fixed in the test kitchen at Big Bob Gibson Bar-B-Q. Although it has never been on the menu, it is a favorite of Big Bob's grandson Don McLemore, and it's a natural pairing with chicken. The sweet vinaigrette dressing makes this dish adaptable to every barbecue region.

Combine the cabbage, onion, bell pepper, celery, and sugar in a large mixing bowl. Mix well and set aside. Combine the vinegar, oil, and salt in a saucepan and bring to a boil. Pour the dressing over the cabbage mixture and stir well. Cover and refrigerate until chilled.

CORN HUSK SKEWERS

SERVES: 4 TO 8

COOKING METHOD:
DIRECT HEAT

SUGGESTED SUPPLIES:
**4 METAL SKEWERS, AT LEAST
12 INCHES LONG**

COOKING TIME: 30 MINUTES

* * * * *

4 EARS OF CORN, IN THE HUSKS

3 ZUCCHINI

8 TABLESPOONS (1 STICK) BUTTER, SOFTENED

3 TABLESPOONS DIJON MUSTARD

1 TABLESPOON FRESH LEMON JUICE

1 TEASPOON DRIED THYME

1 TEASPOON MINCED ONION

½ TEASPOON GARLIC SALT

* * * * *

If there is one food that can eclipse even the barbecuing tradition of chicken in the South, it's corn. We eat it creamed; in succotash, corn pudding, and cornbread; and of course straight up as buttery corn on the cob. As a side dish for smoky grilled chicken, slightly charred grilled corn is perfection.

Corn husk skewers update the old standby; by adding zucchini or other vegetables such as eggplant, a unique vegetable medley is born. Grilling the veggies together in the husks keeps them from burning, steams them soft, and traps the natural moisture within the cob. Imagine your guests' surprise, when the husks are peeled back and instead of a corn cob this grilled vegetable combination is revealed.

Build a charcoal and/or wood fire for direct grilling.

Without detaching them from the corn cob, peel the husks down to uncover the ears of corn and then remove the silk. Cut the ear of corn from the stalk (a small piece of corn can be left on the stalk). Place the corn husks, still attached to the stalk, in a bowl of water to soak (this helps prevent them from charring as the corn grills).

Cut the ears of corn and the zucchini into ¾-inch-thick medallions. Place the vegetables in a medium mixing bowl.

In a small bowl, stir together the softened butter, Dijon mustard, lemon juice, thyme, minced onion, and garlic salt. Blend well and add to the bowl of vegetable medallions. Toss to combine, making sure all of the vegetables are coated well.

Pierce each corn stalk from the bottom with a metal skewer. Thread the vegetables onto the skewer, alternating corn and zucchini. The last vegetable on each skewer should be a corn cob tip. Fold the corn husks back over the vegetables from the bottom up and wrap each ear in aluminum foil.

When the outdoor grill reaches 400°F, cook the foil packets over direct heat for 20 minutes, turning once, then carefully remove the foil and return the skewers to the hot grate. Cook over direct heat for 10 more minutes, turning several times to prevent burning. Remove the skewers from the grill and peel down the husks for a great presentation.

GRILLED FRUIT SKEWERS
with Spicy Maple Cumin Glaze

SERVES: 4 TO 6

COOKING METHOD:
DIRECT HEAT

SUGGESTED SUPPLIES:
4 BAMBOO SKEWERS

COOKING TIME: 3 MINUTES

★ ★ ★ ★ ★

GLAZE

½ CUP PURE MAPLE SYRUP

¼ TEASPOON GROUND CUMIN

¼ TEASPOON GROUND CINNAMON

¼ TEASPOON CAYENNE PEPPER

4 CUPS FRUIT CHUNKS SUCH AS PINEAPPLE,
PEACHES, AND/OR BANANAS

★ ★ ★ ★ ★

Barbecuing gets a bad rap sometimes as being the domain of fatty meats and high-calorie sauces, but the truth of the matter is that smoking and grilling don't add fat to a dish, only flavor. With the right ingredients the outdoor cooker can be the focus of cooking for a healthy diet.

These charcoal-grilled fruit skewers, with their spicy flair, make eating fruit exciting. It's a versatile dessert or side dish recipe that can be made with any number of fruit combinations. Pair it with grilled chicken and enjoy a guilt-free meal.

Build a charcoal fire for direct grilling. Soak the bamboo skewers in a bowl of water and set aside.

Combine the glaze ingredients in a medium bowl and mix well. Add the fruit and toss gently to coat with the glaze. Cover and refrigerate.

Thread the fruit on the soaked skewers, alternating each fruit type. Place the skewers on the grill and cook directly over medium-high heat for 1½ minutes on each side, or until browned and caramelized. Serve warm.

BELL PEPPER BUNDLES

SERVES: 6

**COOKING METHOD:
INDIRECT HEAT**

COOKING TIME: 45 MINUTES

★ ★ ★ ★ ★

3 RED BELL PEPPERS

4½ CUPS SHREDDED CABBAGE

1½ TEASPOONS LAWRY'S SEASONED SALT

12 PATS (TEASPOONS) BUTTER

1 VIDALIA ONION OR SWEET ONION

★ ★ ★ ★ ★

When barbecuing chicken outdoors, it is sometimes easy to focus on the main course and forget about the side dishes. Bell pepper bundles are an easy side dish that can be dropped on the cooker right along with the birds.

Hobo packs—simple aluminum-foil pouches—are a great way to steam vegetables when cooking outdoors. Any vegetables will work with this type of cooking. This red bell pepper, green cabbage, and sweet onion combination not only packs a delicious flavor punch but makes a beautiful presentation. Serve the vegetables right out of the foil for a more rustic look or arrange them on a serving platter.

Build a charcoal and/or wood fire on one side of the grill, leaving the other side void. This will create an area for indirect heat.

Cut the peppers in half through the stems and remove all veins and seeds. Stuff each pepper half with ¾ cup of the shredded cabbage.

Sprinkle each stuffed pepper with seasoned salt and top with a pat of butter. Cut the onion into 6 equal slices. Place an onion slice on each stuffed pepper, top with a second pat of butter, and sprinkle with more seasoned salt. Place each stuffed red pepper on a doubled sheet of aluminum foil. Wrap the peppers and seal tight.

When the grill temperature is at 400°F, place the foil bundles on the grill away from the heat and cook for 45 minutes, or until the peppers are soft. Serve hot.

BIG MAMA'S POUND CAKE

MAKES: 1 CAKE

COOKING METHOD: OVEN

COOKING TIME: 1 HOUR

★　★　★　★　★

2 CUPS SUGAR

1 CUP (2 STICKS) BUTTER, SOFTENED

6 LARGE EGGS, AT ROOM TEMPERATURE

2 CUPS UNSIFTED ALL-PURPOSE FLOUR

1 TABLESPOON PURE VANILLA EXTRACT

★　★　★　★　★

Just like barbecue, the art of making something as simple as pound cake is often forgotten as we are always looking to make things better through the sheer volume of ingredients. Sometimes foods don't need to dazzle to make an impression. Pound cake is best when it acts as a counterbalance to a meal made up of rich flavors.

Big Mama's pound cake supports the "keep it simple, cook it right" approach. How can you go wrong with butter, sugar, eggs, flour, and vanilla? The most important attributes of perfect pound cake are flavor, density, and moisture. Too dense and you sacrifice moisture, too moist and you might as well frost it and break out the candles. Let Big Mama show you how it's done!

Preheat the oven to 300°F. Grease and flour a 12-cup tube pan.

In a medium bowl, combine the sugar and butter and beat well. Add each egg and a portion of flour alternately, beating well after each addition. Stir in the vanilla extract. Pour the batter into the prepared pan and bake for 1 hour, or until the cake turns golden brown and is firm to the touch. Turn onto a cake rack and let it cool for 15 minutes before slicing.

CHAPTER 5

FOUR HOOVES AND A FIRE

★ ★ ★ ★ ★

EARLY SETTLERS IN THE SOUTH RELIED NOT ONLY ON

raising farm animals to provide sustenance but on hunting wild game as well. Hunting was critical to the diet of the settlers and also supplied animal products to be used as tools and for clothing and fabrics. Professional market hunters specialized in trapping and hunting, providing meat for the growing towns.

Through the 1920s and 1930s both raising animals on small farms and hunting for game remained prevalent in North Alabama. After an animal was harvested, it was either butchered on the farm or taken to town to a professional butcher. Of course in Decatur, Alabama, there was a third option: Big Bob Gibson. He solved the problem of how locals could cook a whole animal or their very large cuts of meat.

Although the menu at Big Bob Gibson Bar-B-Q was very limited, food cooked in the kitchen varied greatly on a daily basis. Some of the commerce that took place at the restaurant happened at the back door because you couldn't get away with bringing an armload of fresh raccoons through the front of the restaurant.

★ ★ ★ ★ ★

That's right, the secret is out. Back then Big Bob cooked anything to order, and I mean **anything** that came through the back doors. Venison, ducks, geese, rabbit, armadillo, wild hog, raccoon, beaver, and goat all graced the grates of the smoker at one time or another. If Big Bob didn't have a recipe for a particular varmint, he would make one up, hoping to please his customer.

Big Bob Gibson Bar-B-Q specialized in cooking not only wild game but livestock as well. Local farmers regularly carried whole hogs through the back door, knowing the next day they could pick up a huge mound of succulent pork. Farm-raised goat, rabbit, and lamb were other items that were prepared but never made it to the menu.

This chapter stays true to one of Big Bob's favorite sayings: "All you need is four hooves and a fire." It features cooking whole pig, not only with five different recipes, but with five cooking methods as well. But most important, if you want to try one of these recipes, you're going to need a bigger cooker! A whole pig is not something you can drop on your backyard kettle grill. Remember the old saying "There's more than one way to cook a pig"? Me neither, but it's true. In this chapter you'll find recipes for pig in a direct-fired cooker (North Carolina Pig), pig cooked by indirect heat (Memphis Pig), pig cooked on a spit (Cowboy Pig), and pig cooked with a Caribbean flair (Cuban Pig). If you can't possibly find a big enough cooker, try the whole pig cooked underground (Hawaiian Pig).

Besides whole pig, samplings of some of Big Bob's backdoor favorites are covered in the next bunch of pages, along with a few new enticements. Goat, lamb, and venison can all bring rave reviews when cooked at a low temperature for a long period of time. Using direct heat is the best option for grilling rabbits, as discussed later in the chapter. There is even a recipe for one of the most popular foods at barbecue restaurants in the Southeast, Brunswick stew—a must for cold winter days.

The first customer of Bob Gibson Jr. Pit Bar-B-Q posed for a picture on opening day in 1950. *Overleaf:* Show Hog! A pig cooked in the North Carolina style glistens prior to flipping and a little more cooking.

1950s

The mid-century began the most important decade in Bob Gibson's barbecue legacy. This marked the silver anniversary of his successful barbecue enterprise. The paint was still drying on his new restaurant and business was better than ever. Big Bob the entrepreneur was as happy as a hog in a wallow. Bob Gibson the family man was mired in a pigsty.

Attention to detail was not one of Big Bob's strong points. He did what he did, and then either reaped the benefits or paid the consequences. Many of his decisions were made out of necessity and not of choice. Such was the case when he left his old home place for the last time with signed divorce papers in his hand. The year was 1950, and divorce wouldn't have been too unusual; but he and Big Mama had been separated for twenty-two years!

Big Bob's second marriage, to Annie, lasted for one year, until she passed away in 1951 and left him to run his thriving business alone. He turned to his fifth child, Catherine "Punk" McLemore, to help him through this tough transition. With Punk by his side, Big Bob no longer had to focus on the tedious details of everyday business and was free to do the things he was good at: trading yarns with his customers, cooking barbecue, and casting a jig along the banks of the Tennessee River.

Punk's entry into the business in 1952 was part of a pattern of interest in barbecue among the entire next generation of the Gibson clan. As Decatur grew, Little Bob and Ruth joined in tandem to open their own restaurant, Bob Gibson Jr. Pit Bar-B-Q, in 1950 to satisfy the demand for the Gibsons' slow-smoked flavors. With Big Bob's blessing, Sister and Cotton took the family's trade secrets to Huntsville, Alabama, and established Gibson Barbecue there in 1956. Their efforts defined the flavors of barbecue in that city, and generations later they are still smoking.

Big Bob and Big Mama were married in 1907. Five of their children went on to open barbecue restaurants.

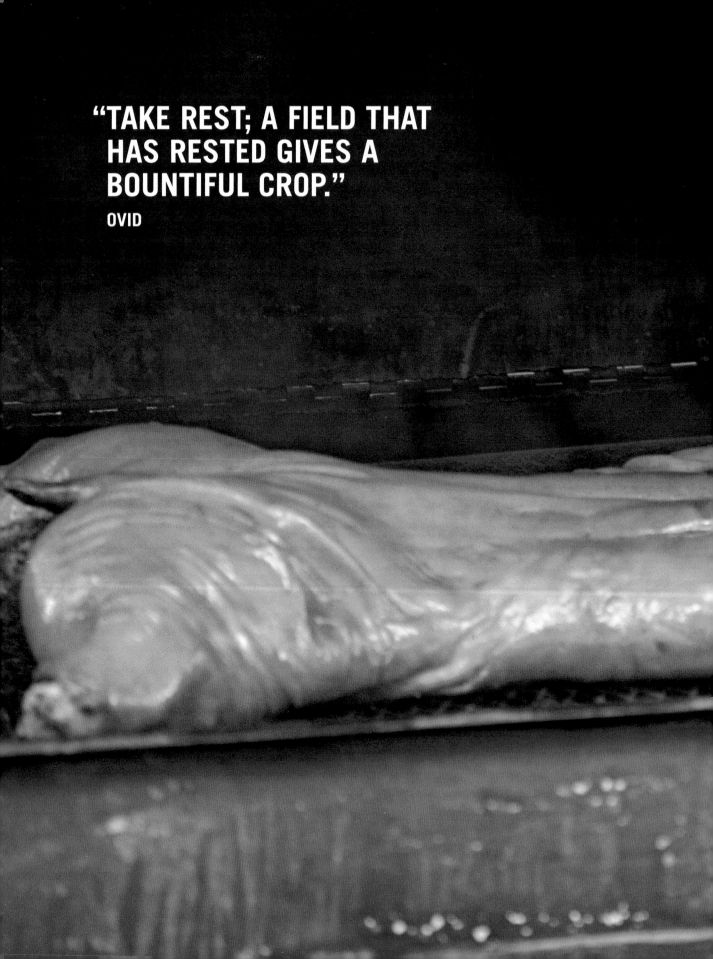

"TAKE REST; A FIELD THAT HAS RESTED GIVES A BOUNTIFUL CROP."
OVID

NORTH CAROLINA PIG

SERVES: 70

COOKING METHOD:
DIRECT HEAT

SUGGESTED WOOD:
HICKORY

SUGGESTED SUPPLIES:
1 SINGLE-CHAMBER DIRECT
COOKER (WITH FIREBOX INSIDE
THE MAIN COOKING CHAMBER),
PLUS AN ADDITIONAL GRILL OR
BURN PIT; 80 POUNDS CHARCOAL
AND WOOD CHUNKS FOR
SEASONING OR ¼ CORD OF WOOD;
2 RECTANGLES OF HEAVY-GAUGE
WIRE FENCING OR GRATE,
SLIGHTLY LARGER THAN THE PIG
BUT SMALLER THAN THE COOKER

COOKING TIME: 8 HOURS

* * * * *

**1 WHOLE DRESSED PIG, BUTTERFLIED, ABOUT
120 POUNDS (SEE PITMASTER'S TIP, PAGE 159)**

1 CUP SALT

**EASTERN CAROLINA PIG PICKIN' SAUCE
(PAGE 221) OR WESTERN CAROLINA PIG DIP
(PAGE 224)**

* * * * *

One of the only places in the world where you can enjoy fresh, chopped whole pig straight from the barbecue cooker is in North Carolina. The tradition of cooking whole hog directly over hickory or oak wood that has been reduced to coals and then soaking the chopped meat with a vinegar-based sauce is one that has been enjoyed since the birth of American-style barbecue.

The first time I experienced this exquisite taste, it was in the North Carolina countryside at a roadside shanty they called a restaurant. The rhythmic beat of the meat cleavers pounding the butcher block echoed through the rafters, and vibrations from the tin roof added harmony to this musical cadence. I stood shoulder-to-shoulder with locals waiting for a table to clear before being handed my greatly anticipated lunch. I watched moist chunks of hand-chopped pig fall from my overstuffed sandwich as I thanked God for North Carolina. Make this in your own backyard and you'll be giving thanks as well.

Place the butterflied pig on a heavy-gauge wire grate, skin side down. Score the meat of the hams and shoulders with a sharp knife; this allows the heat to penetrate. Use the full cup of salt to season the cavity of the hog, working the salt into all the crevices to make sure that all exposed meat is seasoned thoroughly. Flip the pig so it is skin side up on the wire grate.

Light 20 pounds of charcoal in the bottom of the cooker, or if using wood, light 5 medium-size logs. When the charcoal is hot and grayish white or the wood coals are red hot, spread the coals into a barbell-shaped pile approximately the same size as the hog. This allows the thicker portions of the hog (shoulders and hams) to cook hotter and finish cooking at the same time as thinner portions (ribs and loin).

When the coals are ready, grasp the wire grate with the hog on top and transfer it to the cooker. Center the hog over the barbell-shaped charcoal bed.

Opposite: No spatula needed! Flipping the hog should be done with two people and two wire grates. Tie the grates together to prevent a premature pig pickin'.

Recipe continues

When the hog has cooked for 2 hours, start 10 pounds of charcoal or wood in a separate "burn pit." Transfer these hot coals to your primary cooker every hour or so, through the cooker's side access door, during the cooking process to maintain a cooking temperature of 250 to 260°F. Start another 10 pounds of charcoal or wood coals every hour to supplement the coals.

After 4 hours, open the cooker, place the second wire grate over the pig, bind the edges of the wire grates together with rope or wire, and flip the pig. Be warned that this is a two-man operation. With one person standing at each end of the pig, grasp the edges of the grates and turn the pig. Close the cooker lid and cook for an additional 4 hours, or until the internal temperature of the hams and shoulders reach 190 to 195°F.

Let the cooked pig rest for 30 minutes, then bone and chop all the serveable meat, adding the skin if desired (see Pitmaster's Tip). Add your choice of vinegar sauce to the pile of chopped pork to taste, and mix well.

★ PITMASTER'S TIP ★

When cooking North Carolina–style chopped pig, the skin provides a couple of tasty serving options. The chopped meat may be placed back into the hollow, crisp pork skin and served buffet style. The other option would be to chop the crispy skin and add it to the meat to provide extra flavor.

MEMPHIS PIG

SERVES: 70

COOKING METHOD:
INDIRECT HEAT

SUGGESTED WOOD:
HICKORY, PEACH, APPLE

SUGGESTED SUPPLIES:
1 INDIRECT COOKER; 80 POUNDS CHARCOAL AND WOOD CHUNKS FOR SEASONING OR ¼ CORD OF WOOD; 1 ROLL 18-INCH-WIDE HEAVY-DUTY ALUMINUM FOIL

COOKING TIME:
13 HOURS 30 MINUTES TO 14 HOURS 30 MINUTES

★ ★ ★ ★ ★

DRY RUB

1 CUP BROWN SUGAR

¾ CUP SALT

5 TABLESPOONS PAPRIKA

1 TABLESPOON CHILI POWDER

4 TEASPOONS BLACK PEPPER

2 TEASPOONS GARLIC POWDER

1 TEASPOON CAYENNE PEPPER

½ TEASPOON GROUND GINGER

INJECTION

6 CUPS APPLE JUICE

6 CUPS WHITE GRAPE JUICE

7½ CUPS SUGAR

3 CUPS SALT

Although Memphis itself is not noted for whole-pig barbecue, if you ever attend the Memphis in May World Championship Barbecue Cooking Contest, you will be able to get a taste. At this annual event there are three professional meat categories: whole hog, pork shoulder, and pork ribs. It is, after all, billed as "The Super Bowl of Swine."

Over the years, the flavor profile of the winning pigs at Memphis has changed, with the sweet and fruity flavors overtaking the vinegar-based flavors of traditional North Carolina pigs. No one has proved this better than Myron Mixon of the Jack's Old South cooking team, whose peach-wood–smoked pig, layered with flavors from a sweet fruity injection and sweet tomato-based sauce, has consistently put him on the awards podium.

Layering complementary flavors is the key to success on the competition circuit. This recipe features the same sweet, fruity, layered flavors that have historically brought home the bacon at the Memphis.

In a small bowl, combine the dry rub ingredients. Mix well and set aside. In a separate mixing bowl, combine all the injection ingredients and blend until the sugar dissolves.

Remove the cooking grate from the indirect barbecue cooker and cover it with sheets of aluminum foil, letting at least 2 feet of excess foil hang from the edges. Rub the skin of the butterflied pig all over with olive oil. Place the pig on the aluminum foil, skin side down. Using a meat syringe, inject the meat evenly with the entire amount of injection solution. Next, season the cavity of the pig with the dry rub. Work the rub into all crevices and make sure that all the exposed meat is seasoned thoroughly. Bring the excess foil up and over the pig, wrapping it completely.

Light 10 pounds of charcoal in the firebox and add 2 chunks of wood. If using all wood, light 5 logs in the firebox of the indirect cooker. When the cooker reaches 225°F, place the hog and the cooking grate into the cooker. Maintain the cooking temperature by adding 10 pounds of charcoal and 2 chunks of wood every 2 hours or as needed. A more consistent temperature can be held if the charcoal is prelit and graying when added to the firebox. If using all wood, add 2 sticks every 1 to 2 hours.

1 WHOLE DRESSED PIG, BUTTERFLIED, ABOUT 120 POUNDS (SEE PITMASTER'S TIP, PAGE 159)

1 CUP OLIVE OIL

MEMPHIS-STYLE CHAMPIONSHIP RED SAUCE (PAGE 220)

After 11 hours of cooking, tear the aluminum foil to expose the pig. Cook for an additional 2 to 3 hours, until the internal temperature of the hams and shoulders reaches 190 to 195°F. Paint a coat of Memphis-Style Championship Red Sauce on the meat and cook for an additional 30 minutes. Remove the pig from the cooker and let it rest for 30 minutes before hand-pulling the meat.

★ ★ ★ ★ ★

1950s

The mid-1950s were happy times for Big Bob. He was able to look back and appreciate what he had accomplished himself and the direction his children had chosen. He began to patch up some of the strained relationships with his family from the many years of having been absent as a father figure. With a skip in his step he started to enjoy good fortune and then wham! Along came Annie #2.

To describe their relationship—well, let's just say she swept him off his feet . . . immediately! Big Bob and Annie #2 got married with little family fanfare in 1953. It wasn't long before Annie started having direct involvement in the restaurant operations. Their very quick courtship and her immediate advancement into business affairs at the restaurant created tension between Annie #2 and Big Bob's children. They took the view that this woman, who was much younger than Big Bob, was after more than Big Bob's affection. Whoever thought digging for gold in a barbecue pit would be a prosperous venture?

In 1954, Big Bob received a phone call from his longtime banker. The message was, "Get down here now! Your wife is coming to clean you out!" With the vigor of a teenager, Big Bob was out the door and into his pickup truck. They say barbecue wasn't the only thing smoking that day as his tires spun on the hot summer pavement. It was a race to the bank that could only be described as "Cannonball Run." The winner of this grand prix would receive the entire equity surplus of the restaurant and Big Bob's personal nest egg.

The relieved look of the gentleman at the front door of the bank told Big Bob he was the first to arrive. To this day the family does not know if the faithful banker was truly looking out for Big Bob's best interest or if the sweat that drenched his brow was from the potential "beat down" he would have endured if Annie #2 had arrived first. Whatever the case, Big Bob withdrew the accounts on his own. Annie #2 wore a puzzled look on her face as she passed Big Bob in the bank's foyer. No words were spoken, but Big Bob gave her a smug grin and a slight nod of his head as he strolled past her and out the door. When Annie #2 left the bank that day, two things were closed: Big Bob's bank accounts and yet another marriage.

COWBOY PIG

SERVES: 70

COOKING METHOD:
OPEN SPIT

SUGGESTED WOOD:
HICKORY, OAK, PECAN

SUGGESTED SUPPLIES:
1 OPEN SPIT COOKER (SPIT AND HOG ARE VISIBLE DURING COOKING); 100 POUNDS CHARCOAL AND WOOD CHUNKS FOR SEASONING OR ¼ CORD OF WOOD; A SPOOL OF BALING WIRE

COOKING TIME: 10 TO 12 HOURS

★ ★ ★ ★ ★

1 WHOLE DRESSED PIG, POCKET CUT, ABOUT 120 POUNDS (SEE PITMASTER'S TIP, PAGE 159)

1 CUP OLIVE OIL

DRY RUB

1 CUP GRANULATED SUGAR

1 CUP PAPRIKA

⅔ CUP GARLIC SALT

½ CUP BROWN SUGAR

2 TABLESPOONS CHILI POWDER

4 TEASPOONS CAYENNE PEPPER

4 TEASPOONS BLACK PEPPER

2 TEASPOONS DRIED OREGANO

2 TEASPOONS GROUND OCUMIN

BASTE

BARBADO BASTE (PAGE 239)

★ ★ ★ ★ ★

In 2002, I received a phone call from Fast Eddie Maurin, a well-known pitmaster and competition cook from Kansas City. He informed me that MAXIM magazine was doing an article on barbecuing whole pig with three different cooking methods: indirect cooking, underground, and open spit. Eddie told the editors of the magazine to look no further; he had two other experts lined up to help them pull off their three-way pig pickin': Ray Lampe (aka Dr. BBQ) and me. In a gesture that would live up to his nickname, Eddie volunteered to cook one pig in a closed smoker with indirect heat. Now, any true barbecuer can cook a pig on an indirect cooker in his or her sleep, but there would be no sleep for whoever drew the labor-intensive spit. Later that day, the call I was anxiously awaiting came. The editor from MAXIM said, "I heard you were an expert at cooking a pig on an open spit."

Of all possible whole-pig cooking methods, the open spit arguably offers the best atmosphere for an outdoor party. Unlike other cookers, the open spit offers a clear view of the turning pig throughout the entire cook, enticing the crowd with both sights and smells of the barbecue. The spit becomes the centerpiece of conversation while barbecue anticipation builds to a climax.

Check your hog to be sure the pelvis and rib cage are not split entirely. With a meat saw or sharp knife, cut the hooves off at the joint in the middle of the leg.

Rub the skin of the pig all over with the olive oil. This step will keep the skin from charring and promote a rich mahogany color on the cooked skin. In a small bowl, combine the dry rub ingredients. Apply the entire amount of dry rub to all the exposed meat, including under the rib cage. You can't over-season because much of the seasoning will wash out when the pig turns during the cooking process.

Run the spit shaft through the hog's mouth, through the rib cage, and between the hams (thighs) of the hog. The hog should be fastened securely to the shaft so that it rotates when the shaft is turned. Truss the front shanks (the area above the hooves) together with baling wire, and repeat with the rear shanks. A proper spit shaft should have perpendicular spikes that pierce and hold the hams securely when the shanks are wired. The alternative to this type of spit shaft would be a shaft with U bolts securing the spine of the hog above the shoulders and the hams.

Recipe continues

Prior to placing the spit shaft on the cooker base, you will need to build a proper fire. If you are working with an all-wood fire, start out by burning 5 logs to create a bed of hot wood coals. If charcoal is your preference, start with a 20-pound bag. When a hot bed of coals is obtained, place the spit shaft, with the pig attached, on the spit base directly over the fire. The body of the pig should be about 16 to 18 inches above the coals. Spread the coals under the whole pig, forming a barbell-shaped charcoal bed. This will ensure the large cuts of meat (shoulders and hams) are above a hotter fire than the less meaty rib section. The cooking temperature at the base of the shoulders and hams should be around 350°F. The cooking temperature at the base of the chest or back should be around 300°F.

The hog should rotate continuously. If your spit is not equipped with a motor, rotate the pig one quarter turn every 15 minutes.

When the hog has spit-roasted for about 2 hours, start a separate "burn pit" to light charcoal or burn wood to replenish the coals in your primary cooker. Add hot coals throughout the cooking process to maintain a steady temperature under the hog, starting a new batch in the burn pit every hour or so.

When grease starts dripping from the pig, the hot coals will begin to flare up. At this point, rake the coals into a rectangle shape underneath the pig. Rake the coals away from the center of the rectangle and fill the center with sand. The sand will absorb the grease during the cooking process, eliminating flare-ups.

After 4 hours of cooking, begin basting the pig every hour with the Barbado Baste.

Continue to add hot coals around the sand, making sure the biggest piles of burning coal are under the shoulders and hams of the pig. When the internal temperature of the shoulders and hams reaches 185°F (after a total of 10 to 12 hours), remove the pig from the spit. Cooking beyond this temperature will result in the pig breaking apart and falling into the fire. Remove the pig from the spit, bone it, and serve.

★ PITMASTER'S TIP ★

When cooking over an open fire, one of your biggest problems will be the wind affecting your cooking temperature. Do like the cowboys and set up your camp in a way that blocks your fire from the wind. If you are still having problems, a simple sheet of tin can work as a deflector shield.

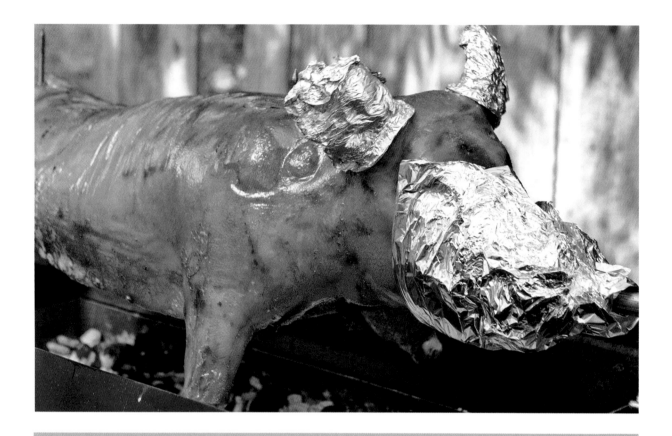

★ PITMASTER'S TIP ★

You're not likely to find a whole pig stacked up in your grocery-store meat case, although with a little notice, your grocery meat manager or favorite butcher should be able to help you out. Be sure to specify "head on" if you desire a "rooter to tooter" presentation. And ask your butcher to cut the pig's hooves off at the first joint below the hams and shoulders. Beyond that, the cooking method or presentation you employ might necessitate additional preparation of the pig. Here's what to ask for.

WHOLE DRESSED PIG (HAWAIIAN)

Ask your butcher for a "whole dressed pig" no matter which cooking style you choose. The pig will come butchered, cleaned, and ready to cook with the breast bone cut, but the rib cage intact. If you want a traditional presentation with the whole pig cooked with the head up, this is your best option.

POCKET-CUT WHOLE DRESSED PIG (COWBOY)

If cooking a pig on a spit is your goal, be sure to specify "pocket cut" when ordering. This means that the breast bone is not cut. A pig that rotates over a hot fire for 8 hours needs all the extra stability it can get. With the rib cage and pelvis intact, your pig will stay on the spit, not fall in the fire.

BUTTERFLIED PIG (NORTH CAROLINA, MEMPHIS, OR CUBAN)

A butterfly cut means the pig's rib are cut as close to the spine as possible. This allows the hog to be spread out and laid flat, or "butterflied," which in turn cuts down the cooking time, allows each piece of meat to cook evenly, and makes it easier to season the meat uniformly.

HAWAIIAN PIG

SERVES: 70

COOKING METHOD:
UNDERGROUND

SUGGESTED SUPPLIES:
¼ CORD OF WOOD OR 160 POUNDS CHARCOAL; 20 TO 30 LARGE RIVER ROCKS 8 TO 10 INCHES IN DIAMETER (FROM A DRY RIVERBED); 10 BURLAP SACKS, SOAKED IN WATER; A 12 X 10-FOOT CANVAS TARP; TWO 4 X 6-FOOT PIECES OF CHICKEN WIRE; A SPOOL OF BALING WIRE; 5 DOZEN BANANA LEAVES OR 10 DOZEN TI LEAVES; SHOVELS

COOKING TIME: 12 HOURS

★ ★ ★ ★ ★

1 WHOLE DRESSED PIG, 120 POUNDS (SEE PITMASTER'S TIP PAGE 159)

½ CUP HAWAIIAN SEA SALT OR KOSHER SALT

¼ CUP SOY SAUCE

1 TABLESPOON GARLIC POWDER

1 TABLESPOON CRACKED BLACK PEPPER

1 TABLESPOON MSG (OPTIONAL)

★ ★ ★ ★ ★

Previous pages: Basting not only flavors the pork and prevents the meat from drying, but fills the air with the most wonderful aroma, building anticipation for the feast.

The Hawaiian Pig can be a great option if your kettle grill and your 125-pound pig don't seem to match. After all, not everyone has a big cooker, but everyone owns a shovel. As Tom Sawyer once said, "Digging the hole can be half the fun"—or something like that. And the moist and tender results from a homemade earthen oven are hard to match with any cooking apparatus.

In Hawaii large volcanic rocks are used to line the **imu,** or underground oven. These rocks hold the heat for an extended period of time, ensuring a proper cook. You can substitute river rocks if they are taken from a "dry" river or creek bed. Rocks from a wet stream have trapped moisture and when they heat they can explode and send shards of sharp rock whistling through the air.

You will also need to find banana leaves and/or ti leaves. Banana trees are often used as ornamental plants for residential landscaping, and leaves can be harvested with no damage to the tree. They are also available frozen in many Latin and Caribbean markets. Ti leaves can be acquired at your local florist, but they can be expensive.

Dig a hole 7 feet long by 4 feet wide by 2½ feet deep. Pile dirt on one side of the pit only. You will be working on the other three sides.

In the center of the pit build a large fire from a quarter cord of wood or 160 pounds of charcoal. When the fire is burning hot, add 20 to 30 large dry river rocks to the fire with a long-handled shovel. Continue to pile more wood or charcoal around and on top of the rocks. The fire is ready for cooking when all the charcoal is lit or the wood forms a bed of hot coals. With a long-handled shovel, make a shallow depression in the middle of the coals and rocks where the pig can lie. Push extra rocks aside and use them later to pile on the sides of the pig.

Lay out one sheet of chicken wire on a table and place the whole pig on top, belly up. Use a sharp knife to score the inside of the hog's hams and shoulders.

In a small bowl, mix the salt, soy sauce, garlic powder, black pepper, and MSG, if using. Rub the seasoning blend evenly on all exposed meat inside and outside of the cavity.

With a long-handled shovel remove 3 to 4 large rocks from the fire and place them into the cavity of the pig. Immediately wrap the pig with the second sheet of chicken wire and secure with baling wire. On each end of the pig, make handles out of baling wire, extending 3 feet from the chicken wire. These will be used to lower your pig and to recover it from the pit.

Place a layer of banana leaves over the hot rocks and coals. Using the baling-wire handles, lower the pig into the pit. Cover the pig with more banana leaves. With the shovel, push extra rocks around all sides of the pig. Cover everything in the pit with the wet burlap sacks. Cover the sacks with the canvas tarp. Starting at the edges of the tarp, cover the whole pit with dirt.

After 12 hours of cooking, unearth the pig. Using the baling wire handles, remove the pig from the pit. Unwrap the chicken wire from the pig and let the pig rest for 30 minutes prior to serving. The pig can either be offered whole, letting the guests use tongs to pull their own meat, or hand-pulled, chopped, and served.

CUBAN PIG

SERVES: 50

COOKING METHOD:
INDIRECT HEAT IN A
SINGLE-CHAMBER COOKER

SUGGESTED WOOD:
HICKORY, OAK, APRICOT

SUGGESTED SUPPLIES:
1 SINGLE-CHAMBER DIRECT
COOKER (WITH FIREBOX INSIDE
THE MAIN COOKING CHAMBER);
80 POUNDS CHARCOAL

COOK TIME: 7 TO 8 HOURS

★ ★ ★ ★ ★

1 WHOLE DRESSED PIG, BUTTERFLIED,
APPROXIMATELY 90 POUNDS (SEE PITMASTER'S
TIP, PAGE 159)

MOJO CRIOLO INJECTION

30 NARANJA AGRIA (SOUR ORANGE) OR SEVILLE
ORANGES (12 CUPS JUICE), OR THE JUICE OF
25 LIMES (3 CUPS), 20 SWEET ORANGES
(8 CUPS), AND 12 LEMONS (1 CUP)

1 CUP EXTRA-VIRGIN OLIVE OIL

1 CUP DARK RUM

¼ CUP GARLIC SALT

8 TEASPOONS SALT

8 TEASPOONS SOY SAUCE

4 TEASPOONS ONION POWDER

RUB

8 HEADS OF GARLIC

1 CUP CHOPPED GREEN ONIONS

5 TABLESPOONS DRIED OREGANO

5 TABLESPOONS BLACK PEPPER

8 TEASPOONS SALT

CARIBBEAN MOJO SAUCE (PAGE 236)

★ ★ ★ ★ ★

One of the highlights in my culinary career was cooking for a Caribbean and Low-Country Food Festival I catered for Johnson & Wales University at the Middleton Place plantation outside of Charleston, South Carolina. We had just won the International Jamaican Jerk Style/Southern Barbecue Cook-Off, and we were invited to cook the Caribbean portion of the menu.

Two 120-pound whole pigs were prepared for the event; one was cooked in the Jamaican jerk style, and the other was prepared Cuban-style with a sour-orange marinade. Once the guests were seated, the pigs were carried from the cooker like ancient royalty in a sedan-chair procession and presented at the head of the buffet. This was the only dinner I have ever attended where the main course, not the chef, got the standing ovation.

I love the intensity and acidity of a sour-orange marinade, and over the years I have tried many ways to get these wonderful flavors dispersed throughout very thick cuts of meat. After much experimentation I've found that two solutions work best: a generous soaking with sour-orange flavors throughout the cooking process or a simple sour-orange injection. With apologies to traditionalists, I chose the latter.

Combine the injection ingredients in a large bowl, and blend well. Place the pig on a tabletop, skin side down. Using a meat syringe, inject the entire amount of injection solution evenly into all of the meat.

To make the rub, separate the cloves from all 8 heads of garlic and peel them. Place the whole garlic cloves, green onions, oregano, pepper, and salt in a food processor and pulse until coarsely chopped. Rub this mixture onto the belly of the pig, working it into all crevices and making sure that all exposed meat is seasoned thoroughly.

Light 20 pounds of charcoal in the bottom of your direct cooker. When the charcoal is hot and grayish white, rake the coals into 4 equal piles in the corners of the cooker. Top each pile of glowing coal with another 5 pounds of unlit charcoal.

Place the pig on the cooker grate skin side down. Center the pig, making sure it does not lie directly over the piles of burning coals.

Recipe continues

Every 2 hours, add 5 pounds more hot charcoal to each pile through the side access door. Cook the pig at 260°F on the covered cooker for 8 hours, or until the internal temperature of the hams and shoulders registers 190°F.

Let the pig rest for 30 minutes prior to serving. The pig can either be offered whole, letting the guests use tongs to pull their own meat, or hand-pulled, chopped, and served. Serve with plenty of Caribbean Mojo Sauce on the side.

Inject the meat evenly with the sour-orange mixture. Cover all exposed meat with the coarse rub, pressing it into the crevices. This will ensure more flavor and moisture both inside and on the outside of the meat.

★ PITMASTER'S TIP ★

If you want to serve the pig with a traditional apple in its mouth, cook the pig with its mouth pried open. A stick about the same length as the diameter of the apple works well. When the pig is cooked, replace the stick with a raw apple.

BARBECUE GOAT

SERVES: 20

COOKING METHOD:
INDIRECT HEAT

SUGGESTED WOOD:
HICKORY, OAK, PECAN

SUGGESTED SUPPLIES:
40 POUNDS CHARCOAL

COOKING TIME: 8 TO 9 HOURS

★ ★ ★ ★ ★

1 WHOLE DRESSED GOAT, BUTTERFLIED,
APPROXIMATELY 20 POUNDS

⅓ CUP SALT

3 TABLESPOONS BLACK PEPPER

BARBADO BASTE (PAGE 239)

★ ★ ★ ★ ★

Though goat is not usually offered at Big Bob's, it has made at least one notable appearance on the menu.

In 1938 the early spring brought on a record crop of wild onion that blanketed the front yard of Big Mama's house. Since separating from Big Bob, she had become responsible not only for raising the children but for pulling up the onions, as well. As she bent over to address this spring nuisance, she presented Ruth's pet goat an irresistible target; taking a running start, the goat sent Big Mama sprawling into the onion patch.

That was the final straw for Big Mama. They loaded the goat into the car and took it straight to Big Bob. The goat didn't have a prayer. But it was quite tasty that day . . . and still is if it's cooked right!

Place the goat, skin side down, on a tabletop. Season the belly of the goat with the salt and pepper, working the seasoning into all crevices and making sure that all exposed meat is coated well.

Light 10 pounds of charcoal in the cooker firebox and add 2 chunks of wood. When the cooker reaches 225°F, place the goat on the grate of the cooker, skin side down. Maintain the cooking temperature by adding 10 pounds of charcoal and 2 chunks of wood every 2 hours or as needed. A more consistent temperature can be held if the charcoal is prelit in a separate burn pit before being added to the firebox.

When the goat has cooked for 3 hours, baste the goat generously with Barbado Baste. Cook, basting every hour, for an additional 5 to 6 hours, or until the internal temperature of the thickest part of the legs reaches 190°F.

Let the goat rest for 20 minutes prior to serving. Drizzle with Barbado Baste prior to serving. The goat can either be offered whole, letting the guests use tongs to pull their meat, or hand-pulled, chopped, and served.

BRUNSWICK STEW

MAKES: 1¼ GALLONS

SERVES: 10 TO 12

COOKING METHOD: STOVE

**COOKING TIME:
3 HOURS 45 MINUTES**

★ ★ ★ ★ ★

1 3.5-POUND PORK BUTT OR BONE-IN PORK SHOULDER ROAST

1 4-POUND WHOLE CHICKEN

3 GALLONS WATER

2 CUPS DICED PEELED POTATOES

3 TEASPOONS SALT

1 TEASPOON BLACK PEPPER

½ TEASPOON GARLIC POWDER

½ TEASPOON CAYENNE PEPPER

2 BEEF BOUILLON CUBES

1 CUP DICED ONIONS

1 10-OUNCE PACKAGE FROZEN BABY LIMA BEANS

1 10-OUNCE PACKAGE FROZEN CORN

2 28-OUNCE CANS CRUSHED TOMATOES

½ CUP KETCHUP

1 TABLESPOON PREPARED YELLOW MUSTARD

1 TABLESPOON BROWN SUGAR

2 TEASPOONS WORCESTERSHIRE SAUCE

1 TEASPOON FRESH LEMON JUICE

★ ★ ★ ★ ★

The great Georgia humorist Roy Blount Jr. once joked, "Brunswick stew is what happens when small mammals carrying ears of corn fall into barbecue pits." The origin of this thick stewed concoction is debatable, but most trace it back to 1828 in Brunswick, Georgia. Brunswick stew is a thick vegetable stew with shredded meat that is cooked over low heat in a large pot. Traditionally, it was made from squirrel or sometimes rabbit, and it has always been a popular way for hunters to make a complete meal from their wild game.

Today, Brunswick stew is popular across the Southeast, although the squirrel and rabbit are generally replaced with pork, chicken, and beef. The vegetables might include corn, onions, tomatoes, beans, squash, or okra. Often it is the feast for large gatherings, festivals, and fund-raisers.

Place the pork and chicken in a large stockpot with the water. Bring to a boil over medium heat. Reduce the heat and cook at a slight boil for 3 hours, or until the pork is tender. Remove the meat to a platter and let cool. When cool enough to handle, bone the meat, discard fat and skin, and chop into small pieces.

Using a large spoon, skim the grease from the top of the stock. Measure 10 cups of stock and pour into a medium pot. Reserve the remaining stock. Add the diced potatoes, salt, black pepper, garlic powder, cayenne pepper, and beef bouillon to the stock and bring to a boil. Cook for 10 minutes, then add the onions, beans, and corn to the pot. When the liquid returns to the boil, cook for an additional 5 to 10 minutes, or until the potatoes are tender.

Reduce the heat and add the reserved meat, crushed tomatoes, ketchup, mustard, brown sugar, Worcestershire, and lemon juice. Simmer for 30 minutes, stirring frequently. If the stew becomes too thick, add a little of the reserved stock. Serve warm.

"AS LONG AS THERE IS WATER AND SODA CRACKERS WE WILL NEVER RUN OUT OF STEW!"

BIG BOB GIBSON

SMOKED VENISON
with White Sauce

SERVES: 10 TO 12

COOKING METHOD:
INDIRECT HEAT

SUGGESTED WOOD:
HICKORY, OAK, CHERRY

COOKING TIME: 9 HOURS

★ ★ ★ ★ ★

1 VENISON HINDQUARTER (12 TO 15 POUNDS)

½ CUP VEGETABLE OIL, OLIVE OIL, OR MELTED LARD

DRY RUB

1 TABLESPOON KOSHER SALT

2 TEASPOONS CHILI POWDER

2 TEASPOONS GARLIC POWDER

2 TEASPOONS BROWN SUGAR

4 PEELED POTATOES, CUT IN QUARTERS

3 ONIONS, CUT IN HALF

3 CARROTS, CUT IN LARGE CHUNKS

8 CUPS BIG BOB GIBSON BAR-B-Q WHITE SAUCE (PAGE 218)

★ ★ ★ ★ ★

If Big Bob Gibson was nowhere to be found at the restaurant, there was a good chance he would be on the lake or in the woods. An avid outdoorsman, he enjoyed not only hunting and fishing, but also cooking his catch. He passed this love of the outdoors on to his kids, especially Cotton, who would leave for the family hunting camp in mid-October and return home in February.

As word spread of Big Bob's smoked venison with white sauce, hunters started dropping their fresh deer meat by the restaurant to have it cooked. During hunting season, venison appeared with regularity on the pits. This dish, similar to a large pot roast with chunks of tender vegetables, is a favorite of local hunters. To this day, the rich aroma of venison can sometimes be smelled in the kitchens of Big Bib Gibson Bar-B-Q, especially during the fall and winter months of hunting season.

Build a fire (wood or a combination of charcoal and wood) for indirect cooking by situating the coals on only one side of the grill, leaving the other side void.

Hand trim the silver membrane, or silver skin, from the venison hindquarter. Coat the venison with ¼ cup of the oil. In a small bowl, mix the dry rub ingredients together, and apply a coat to the entire hindquarter.

When the cooker reaches 250°F, place the venison over the void section of the grill and cook for 4 hours.

Transfer the venison to a large roasting pan and coat with the remaining ¼ cup of oil. Arrange large chunks of potatoes, onions, and carrots around the venison. Pour the white sauce over the meat and cover the pan tightly with aluminum foil. Finish cooking at 250°F for 5 hours. Let the meat rest, covered, at room temperature for 30 minutes prior to serving.

GRILLED RABBIT
with Apple Cider Brine

SERVES: 6 TO 8

**COOKING METHOD:
DIRECT HEAT**

**BRINING TIME:
6 TO 12 HOURS**

COOKING TIME: 40 MINUTES

★　★　★　★　★

APPLE CIDER BRINE

2 CUPS WATER

2 CUPS APPLE CIDER

2½ TABLESPOONS KOSHER SALT

1 TABLESPOON SUGAR

1 TABLESPOON CRACKED BLACK PEPPER

½ TABLESPOON DRIED THYME

½ TEASPOON MINCED GARLIC

6 DRIED ALLSPICE BERRIES

½ BAY LEAF

3 WHOLE RABBITS, SPLIT, 2 POUNDS EACH,
OR 8 RABBIT HIND LEG QUARTERS

BASTING SAUCE

½ CUP SOY MARINADE (PAGE 237)

¼ CUP FRESH LEMON JUICE

3 TABLESPOONS DIJON MUSTARD

3 TABLESPOONS BUTTER

★　★　★　★　★

Rabbits were a special treat for Big Bob Gibson, and even more than hunting them, he enjoyed cooking them. His favorite recipes included rabbit stew, Brunswick stew, and smoked rabbit with white sauce. Sometimes he would let the assigned pitman of the day cook the rabbits in whatever way he wanted to. A cook truly knew he was accepted when Big Bob would just toss his kill on the stainless-steel table and say, "Cook 'em," with no further instruction. The following is a "cook 'em" recipe.

Combine the brine ingredients in a small bowl or resealable plastic bag. Add the rabbit pieces, cover or seal, and refrigerate for 6 to 12 hours.

Combine the basting sauce ingredients in a small nonreactive pan and mix well. Place over medium heat until the mixture is warm. Remove from the heat.

Build a charcoal and/or wood fire with the cooking rack 6 to 8 inches above the coals. Lightly oil the hot grate. When the temperature reaches 350°F, grill the rabbit for 20 minutes on each side, or until the internal temperature reaches 160 degrees. Baste the rabbit liberally with the basting sauce as it grills. Cut the whole rabbit into quarters before serving.

★ PITMASTER'S TIP ★

Cooking "bone-in" lean meats such as rabbit directly over high heat is tricky. High heat will dry the outside meat before the inside meat is cooked through. When cooking lean bone-in cuts, remember to raise the cooking grate above the fire or switch to an indirect cooking method. Also, all lean meat needs protection from the flame, the easiest being an oil-based marinade or baste.

SPICY CUBAN BLACK BEANS AND RICE

SERVES: 8

COOKING METHOD: STOVE

COOKING TIME: 30 MINUTES

★ ★ ★ ★ ★

⅓ CUP OLIVE OIL

1 GREEN BELL PEPPER, CORED, SEEDED, AND CHOPPED

1 JALAPEÑO PEPPER OR AJI CACHUCHA PEPPER, SEEDED AND CHOPPED

1 ONION, CHOPPED

7 GARLIC CLOVES, MINCED

1 TABLESPOON DRIED OREGANO

1 BAY LEAF

1 TEASPOON SALT

¾ TEASPOON GROUND CUMIN

½ TEASPOON BLACK PEPPER

½ TEASPOON CAYENNE PEPPER

4 CUPS BLACK BEANS SOAKED OVERNIGHT IN WATER, OR DRAINED CANNED BEANS

¾ CUP WATER OR CHICKEN STOCK

3 CUPS PREPARED RICE

★ ★ ★ ★ ★

What better side dish to serve beside Cuban Pig (page 165) than **moros y cristianos**, or black beans and rice? Black beans are a staple of Cuban cooking, used in soups, stews, and sauces. Black beans can be traced back 7,000 years to southern Mexico and Central America, and their popularity has spread throughout the Caribbean and the southern United States, especially the Southwest and Florida. This spicy and filling recipe breaks the mold on traditional barbecue side dishes but can also be served as a complete meal.

Add the olive oil to a large pan over medium heat. Add the bell pepper, jalapeño pepper, onion, and garlic and sauté for 3 minutes, then add the oregano, bay leaf, salt, cumin, black pepper, and cayenne pepper. Sauté until the vegetables soften, then turn the heat to low. Mash 1 cup of the beans to a paste and add to vegetable mixture. Add the remaining whole beans and the water or chicken stock. Simmer until the mixture thickens, about 20 minutes. Serve over the hot cooked rice.

BARBECUE LAMB SHANKS

SERVES: 4

COOKING METHOD:
INDIRECT HEAT

SUGGESTED WOOD:
HICKORY, PECAN, OAK

MARINATING TIME:
12 HOURS

COOKING TIME:
1 HOUR 15 MINUTES

★ ★ ★ ★ ★

SEASONING PASTE

1½ TABLESPOONS SALT

1 TABLESPOON PAPRIKA

3¾ TEASPOONS BLACK PEPPER

2¼ TEASPOONS GARLIC POWDER

¾ TEASPOON DRIED THYME

¾ TEASPOON DRIED ROSEMARY

¾ TEASPOON DRIED OREGANO

¾ TEASPOON GROUND GINGER

3 TABLESPOONS EXTRA-VIRGIN OLIVE OIL

2 TABLESPOONS SOY SAUCE

2 TABLESPOONS DIJON MUSTARD

1 TABLESPOON FRESH LEMON JUICE

4 LAMB SHANKS

★ ★ ★ ★ ★

The essence of barbecue is taking the cheapest cuts of meat and turning them into succulent dishes by cooking them at a lower temperature. Take lamb, for example. The very desirable leg portion of lamb can be purchased in most supermarkets at a premium price. The less meaty shank portion costs much less and will still draw raves at the dinner table. Lamb shanks, cut from the lower portion of the leg, are sold bone-in, in about one-pound portions. Allow one shank per person.

In a food processor, combine the salt, paprika, black pepper, garlic powder, thyme, rosemary, oregano, and ginger. Pulse until the herbs are lightly ground. Add the olive oil, soy sauce, Dijon mustard, and lemon juice and blend until the mixture forms a paste.

Hand trim any silver membrane or silver skin from the lamb shanks. Coat the shanks with the seasoning paste, place in a plastic storage bag, and refrigerate for 12 hours.

Build a fire (wood or a combination of charcoal and wood) for indirect cooking by situating the coals on only one side of the grill, leaving the other side void. When the cooker reaches 250°F, place the lamb shanks on the void section of the grill. Cook for 1 hour and 15 minutes, or until the internal temperature of the lamb reaches 125°F for rare, 135°F for medium-rare, or 145°F for medium. Let the lamb rest for at least 15 minutes before serving.

BIG BOB GIBSON BAR-B-Q COLESLAW

SERVES: 6 TO 8

★ ★ ★ ★ ★

1 LARGE HEAD OF GREEN CABBAGE
¾ CUP SUGAR
1 TABLESPOON SALT
¾ CUP DISTILLED WHITE VINEGAR

★ ★ ★ ★ ★

Coleslaw is probably the side dish most often associated with barbecue, and its simple flavors match so well with smoked meat. The most common varieties include vinegar-based, mayonnaise-based, and mustard-based.

Big Bob Gibson realized the harmonious relationship between slaw and barbecue early on. When he opened his first restaurant, vinegar slaw and Golden Flake potato chips were his only side-dish offerings, and a sweet tangy scoop of his coleslaw graced every barbecue sandwich that left the kitchen. As he told his customers, "If ya don't like slaw, scrape it off!" Very little has changed in more than eighty years at the restaurant, including Big Bob's original coleslaw recipe.

With a sharp knife, cut the cabbage in quarters and core. Then cut the cabbage to a fine dice. Place the cabbage, sugar, and salt in a large bowl and toss to mix. Add the vinegar, and stir well. This slaw can be served at room temperature or chilled.

BIG MAMA'S CHOW-CHOW

MAKES: 3 PINTS

SERVES: 8 TO 10

COOKING METHOD: STOVE

STANDING TIME: 4 TO 12 HOURS

COOKING TIME: 1 HOUR

★ ★ ★ ★ ★

1 MEDIUM HEAD OF CABBAGE, CORED AND SHREDDED

4 GREEN BELL PEPPERS, CORED, SEEDED, AND DICED

2 ONIONS, DICED

2 GREEN TOMATOES OR 5 HUSKED TOMATILLOS, DICED

½ CUP SALT

3 CUPS DISTILLED WHITE VINEGAR

2½ CUPS SUGAR

1 TABLESPOON CELERY SEED

1 TEASPOON GROUND TURMERIC

★ ★ ★ ★ ★

Chow-chow is a pickled vegetable dish that is served cold as a side dish or condiment. Its name comes from the French word **chou**, meaning cabbage, and the ingredients almost always include cabbage; but asparagus, beans, carrots, cauliflower, and peas can be added, as well.

Big Mama's recipe has a Pennsylvania Dutch influence. It is sweeter than most Southern varieties, and it matches well with all types of barbecue and foods off the grill. Her favorite way to serve it was as a side dish—an alternative to slaw; but it makes a great topper for barbecue sandwiches, hamburgers, and hot dogs. For breakfast, chow-chow makes a flavorful addition to scrambled eggs and biscuits and gravy.

In a medium nonreactive stockpot, combine the cabbage, bell peppers, onions, and tomatoes (the raw vegetables should equal 2½ to 3 quarts). Stir in the salt, cover the pot, and let the vegetables stand at room temperature for 4 to 12 hours. Drain well in a colander.

Rinse the pot and add the vinegar, sugar, celery seed, and turmeric. Bring to a boil. Add the drained vegetables, return to a boil, then reduce the heat and simmer for 1 hour stirring occasionally. Serve hot or cold.

DRIED APPLES

MAKES: 4 CUPS

COOKING METHOD: OVEN

COOKING TIME: 6 TO 8 HOURS

★ ★ ★ ★ ★

2 TABLESPOONS FRESH LEMON JUICE

2 CUPS WATER

8 APPLES, PEELED, CORED, AND CUT IN ¼-INCH-THICK SLICES

★ ★ ★ ★ ★

In the Depression years, it was not uncommon to see little Sara Ruth Gibson haul a pillowcase loaded with fresh sliced apples onto the barn roof. Sara Ruth was the smallest and most agile of the Gibson children, so the job of drying apples was assigned to her. She would spread the pillowcase flat on the tin roof and spread the apples in a single layer inside her makeshift white tote bag. For five days she would put the apples out in the morning and fetch them at sundown, a ritual that could only mean one thing: Big Mama would be baking Apple Rolls with Vanilla Sauce that week.

Dried apples make a great snack by themselves, or they can be stored and refreshed for use in cakes, pies, cobblers, and applesauce. Any type of apple can be dried as long as it is firm and not overripe. If a tin-roofed barn is not available at your home for drying, the oven can be used successfully.

Preheat the oven to 150°F.

Combine the lemon juice and water in a large bowl and add the apple slices; this will keep the apples from oxidizing and turning brown. Drying them without dipping them in this acidic mixture will cause the apples to turn slightly brown but will in no way affect the taste.

Arrange the apple slices on wire cake racks in a single layer, making sure not to overlap the edges. Air circulation around the apple slices is important when drying. Using a cookie sheet will work, but the apples will need to be flipped several times during the drying process. Bake for 6 to 8 hours, rotating the racks once during the cooking process for more uniform dried apples. The apples should be flexible and not brittle when removed from the oven. The surface of the apples should be dry, not wet or tacky.

Let the apples cool for 30 minutes and then store in a vacuum-sealed bag or a plastic storage bag with the air removed. Dried apples will keep for 6 to 8 months or longer if frozen.

APPLE ROLLS
with Vanilla Sauce

SERVES: 8

COOKING METHOD: OVEN

**COOKING TIME:
1 HOUR 35 MINUTES**

★ ★ ★ ★ ★

4 CUPS DRIED APPLES (PAGE 179)

3¾ CUPS WATER

½ CUP SUGAR

APPLE ROLL DOUGH

3½ CUPS SIFTED ALL-PURPOSE FLOUR

1½ TEASPOONS SALT

1 CUP PLUS 2 TABLESPOONS SHORTENING

10 TABLESPOONS COLD WATER, OR MORE AS
NEEDED

VANILLA SAUCE

3 CUPS MILK

2 EGGS

½ CUP SUGAR

2 TABLESPOONS ALL-PURPOSE FLOUR

¼ TEASPOON SALT

1 TABLESPOON BUTTER

1 TEASPOON PURE VANILLA EXTRACT

1 EGG, BEATEN

★ ★ ★ ★ ★

Big Mama always had a large supply of dried apples on hand for recipes like this one. It was a family favorite because these simple flavors could be served with almost anything.

When researching this particular dish with the family, very different memories surfaced regarding the crust. Some remembered the apple rolls having a very puffy dough crust, while some remembered it being thin and flaky. After pondering this conundrum, I concluded that Big Mama made this recipe to use up leftover dough; the crust would vary depending on whether she had been making biscuits, pie shells, or rolls. This is only a hypothesis, but I encourage you to try all three types of dough for these delicious apple rolls!

Place the dried apples and the water in a large saucepan. Bring to a boil, lower the heat to medium, and simmer for 1 hour. Stir occasionally for the first 45 minutes, then continuously for the last 15 minutes. When the water has evaporated and the apples are softened, add the sugar and stir vigorously, breaking the apple pieces into a chunky paste. Cook for an additional 5 minutes and set aside.

To make the dough, sift the flour into a medium mixing bowl. Add the salt and shortening and use a pastry blender or 2 knives to cut the shortening into the flour until it resembles small peas. Add approximately 10 tablespoons of cold water, 1 tablespoon at a time, mixing well with a small portion of the flour-shortening mixture. When the entire mixture is slightly moist and doughy, separate the dough into 2 equal balls. On a lightly floured work surface, roll each ball into an 8 x 12-inch rectangle, ⅛ inch thick.

Spread 1½ cups of the apple mixture evenly onto each rectangle, leaving 1½ inches of the edges uncovered. Fold the long sides of the pastry toward the center of the filling and loosely lap the edges together to form a log. Fold the two ends of the pastry and pinch them to close.

Place each apple roll onto a greased cookie sheet. Brush the top of each roll lightly with the beaten egg. Bake at 400°F for 35 minutes, or until the crust turns golden brown.

While the apple rolls are baking, begin making the vanilla sauce. Heat 2½ cups of the milk to a very warm temperature in a medium-large saucepan. In a medium bowl, beat the eggs and add the remaining ½ cup of milk. Pour the warm milk into the

egg-milk mixture and stir together. Pour back into the saucepan, and heat over medium-low heat. In a separate bowl, stir together the sugar, flour, and salt. Add to the warm milk-egg mixture and cook, stirring constantly, for 40 minutes, or until the mixture thickens. Add the butter and vanilla, reduce the heat to low, and keep warm until ready to use.

When the apple rolls have cooled, cut into 3-inch portions and serve topped with a ladle of vanilla sauce.

CHAPTER 6

RACK
OF
RIBS

★ ★ ★ ★ ★

IN THE EARLY 1800S, MOST HOGS WERE RAISED BY

individuals who slaughtered them only as the meat was needed. By the mid-1800s, commercial butchering began when the population of towns increased. Hogs were only harvested in cold weather. Their fat was rendered into lard and the meat was cut into sections: shoulders, hams, and sides. These sections of meat were covered in salt and packed in wooden barrels. It was when these barrels of pork were opened and sold that the pork-cut bias began.

The large meaty cuts of ham, shoulder, and loin brought a premium price, but portions of the side, such as ribs, were viewed as cast-off cuts. Pork ribs were consumed by people who couldn't afford to buy the meatier cuts.

This little bit of meatpacking history provides us with a clue as to why barbecue is rooted in the lives of the poor and not the well-to-do. Barbecue is the process of taking the worst cuts of meat and, through a process of cooking at a low temperature with hot coals for an extended period of time, producing tender, flavorful results.

★ ★ ★ ★ ★

Pork ribs did not become a part of the Big Bob Gibson Bar-B-Q menu until the late 1970s. By that time the price of ribs had come full circle and exceeded the cost of ham and shoulders. Decatur, Alabama, continued to grow as more people arrived in the city because of new industry along the Tennessee River. More people meant new customers, and the demand for items on the menu began to shift. Customers from other areas of the country believed that barbecue meant ribs, so the demand for this pork product at Big Bob's skyrocketed.

When it comes to plating barbecue for service, ribs make the perfect presentation. The rich brown of beef ribs or the deep mahogany color of pork ribs are beacons to a hungry man's eyes. Maybe it's the primal instinct to gnaw meat off the bone that makes eating ribs such a viscerally satisfying experience.

There are several different types of pork ribs, each cut from a different part of the rib cage; spare, loin back (baby back), and country-style are the three most popular cuts. They vary in bone size, bone curvature, amount of meat, and fat content, and when cooked they will have slight differences in taste and texture. Often the type of cuisine you are cooking will determine which kind of rib you select.

Unlike other whole cuts of pork, the pork rib is relatively thin, which is a big advantage when it comes to seasoning the meat because you can drive flavors throughout the entire rib in a relatively short period of time. This can be accomplished through a dry rub, marinade, baste, or any combination of seasonings. The thinness of the meat on a rib also allows the smoke flavor to permeate the entire rib.

Along with pork ribs you will find a variety of rib types discussed in this chapter. Beef short ribs and braised back ribs are two recipes that highlight the depth of flavor found in beef, while adding techniques to tenderize these traditional tough cuts. Rack of lamb will take your barbecue to the next level when this deluxe special-occasion meat comes off the grill.

1970s

Although Big Bob Gibson's life was filled with many trials and tribulations, he ultimately succeeded as both a family man and a businessman. His children followed in his footsteps and are still carrying on the tradition and family name in Decatur and Huntsville, Alabama. Big Bob's later years were happy times that he spent fishing and with his fourth wife, Birdie. Big Bob Gibson never retired; he worked until his death in 1972, albeit on his own schedule!

1970s AND '80s

The 1970s and '80s ushered in a growing demand for barbecue and a new generation at Big Bob Gibson Bar-B-Q. Don McLemore, grandson of Big Bob, and his wife, Carolyn McLemore, took control of the Decatur landmark, and under their guidance, the long-unchanged menu took on a new look. In the '70s and '80s three new items were added to quench the desire of new customers. Carolyn rounded out the side-order options with her homemade barbecue baked beans, and the addition of barbecue-stuffed potatoes was a huge success. The giant spuds, once compared to "a Nimitz-class aircraft carrier" by *Chile Pepper* magazine, were filled with butter, sour cream, cheese, bacon, and chives and topped with barbecue. But perhaps no other menu item won more immediate approval than the pork ribs. These meltingly tender specimens, which spent a full 5 hours kissing the hickory coals at 225°F, were introduced in 1978 and have since become a Big Bob's mainstay.

It takes teamwork to make 750 pies the day before Thanksgiving. Don and Carolyn McLemore check the filling while Evelyn Harvel, an employee for fifty-three years, adds meringue to a lemon icebox pie.

MEMPHIS DRY RIBS

SERVES: 4 TO 6

COOKING METHOD:
INDIRECT HEAT

SUGGESTED WOOD:
HICKORY, OAK

COOKING TIME:
4 HOURS

★   ★   ★   ★   ★

2 SLABS ST. LOUIS–CUT PORK SPARERIBS

DRY RUB

10 TEASPOONS DARK BROWN SUGAR

3 TABLESPOONS PAPRIKA

1 TABLESPOON BLACK PEPPER

1 TABLESPOON GARLIC SALT

2 TEASPOONS KOSHER SALT

1 TEASPOON CHILI POWDER

½ TEASPOON ONION POWDER

½ TEASPOON CAYENNE PEPPER

½ TEASPOON GROUND CUMIN

½ TEASPOON DRIED OREGANO

½ TEASPOON RUBBED SAGE

½ TEASPOON DRIED MARJORAM

½ TEASPOON DRIED PARSLEY

¼ TEASPOON WHITE PEPPER

1 CUP WHITE VINEGAR

★   ★   ★   ★   ★

It is impossible to discuss Memphis barbecue without talking about ribs. Where in most places the rib-loving factions are divided between those who prefer baby backs to spareribs (or vice versa), in Memphis the two different camps are partisans of either dry or wet preparations. Wet ribs are daubed with sauce before serving. Dry ribs can have either a dry rub added prior to cooking or a seasoning blend applied after cooking. Either way, no tomato-based sauce touches a dry rib from Memphis.

Remove the membrane from the back of the ribs. Combine the dry rub ingredients and mix well. Reserve ⅓ cup of the dry rub, then apply the remaining rub generously to the front and back of the ribs. Pat gently to ensure the rub adheres to the meat.

Build a fire (wood or a combination of charcoal and wood) for indirect cooking by situating the coals on only one side of the grill, leaving the other side void. Preheat the charcoal grill to 250°F. Place the ribs meat side up on the grill and cook with indirect heat, with the grill lid closed, for 4 hours, or until the ribs are tender.

Mix the vinegar with 1 cup of water in a shallow baking pan. Remove the ribs from the grill and dip them into the vinegar water. Remove the ribs from the wash and place them on a cutting board. Season the ribs immediately with a heavy coat of the reserved dry rub. Cut and serve.

Q: Does boiling ribs prior to barbecuing increase tenderness?

A: Boiling ribs is usually done as a shortcut to produce the tenderness that is achieved through long, slow cooking. Boiling ribs and finishing them on a hot grill will cut the cook time in half. The problem with boiling is the loss of flavor. When you boil the meat, flavor is leached from the meat into the water. You would be better off using the proven low and slow method of barbecuing with indirect heat. Your results will be a more tender and flavorful rib.

1980s

In 1987, a pit fire gutted Big Bob Gibson Bar-B-Q. It was devastating to the family, but it also presented a new opportunity. A new restaurant was built with an expanded kitchen and dining room. An advertising campaign to promote catering was devised to target a large unfulfilled market, and these new facilities were immediately put to good use. Annual catering jobs for more than three thousand people became a routine. A veteran crew and an assembly-line approach to fixing plates made serving large groups both fast and efficient. This improved on Big Bob Gibson's catering technique, which was to pile pork, slaw, and white bread on paper plates and stack them up until the crowds arrived (see pages 6 and 7). His rule of efficient service was not to stack the fixed plates more than five high because they could tip over and cause unnecessary waste.

A sandwich containing a heaping mound of pulled pork, topped with vinegar slaw, is served bundled in a wax-paper wrap.

BIG BOB GIBSON BAR-B-Q RIBS
(well . . . sort of)

SERVES: 4 TO 6

COOKING METHOD:
INDIRECT HEAT

SUGGESTED WOOD:
HICKORY

COOKING TIME:
4 HOURS 20 MINUTES

★ ★ ★ ★ ★

2 SLABS ST. LOUIS–CUT PORK SPARERIBS

DRY RUB

2 TABLESPOONS BROWN SUGAR

1 TABLESPOON PAPRIKA

1½ TEASPOONS KOSHER SALT

1 TEASPOON BLACK PEPPER

½ TEASPOON GARLIC SALT

½ TEASPOON ONION SALT

¼ TEASPOON CELERY SALT

½ TEASPOON CAYENNE PEPPER

½ TEASPOON GROUND CUMIN

MEMPHIS-STYLE CHAMPIONSHIP RED SAUCE
(PAGE 220)

★ ★ ★ ★ ★

Over the years the rib recipe at Big Bob Gibson Bar-B-Q has changed many times, running the gamut from full-size spare ribs to today's meaty St. Louis–cut spare ribs. The seasoning and the sauce have evolved as well, moving from salt and pepper to a complex seasoning blend and a finishing touch of our own championship red sauce.

Spare ribs are cut from the lower portion of the rib cage below the back ribs, including a portion of the breast bone. The bones of the spare rib vary in size and length, ranging from short and round to long and flat, and they have less curvature than baby back ribs. The meat contains a high percentage of fat and thus yields a tender finished product.

The term "St. Louis cut" is used when the breast bone and cartilage are cut from a spare rib, leaving a slab of ribs with a more uniform size and shape. The breast bone can be used for stock, and the leftover meat and cartilage can be seasoned and cooked for rib tips. A full-size spare rib can be trimmed easily at home, or your local butcher can trim the rib and give you the bonus cuttings.

The recipe that follows is as close to what we use at the restaurant as I can give without being disowned by the family. I think you will recognize the similarities—and perhaps even like it better!

Remove the membrane from the back of the ribs. In a small bowl, combine the dry rub ingredients and mix well. Apply generously to the front and back of the ribs, patting gently to ensure the rub adheres.

Build a fire (wood or a combination of charcoal and wood) for indirect cooking by situating the coals on only one side of the grill, leaving the other side void. If using a charcoal cooker, preheat it to 250°F. Place the ribs on the grill meat side up and cook with indirect heat for 4 hours, or until the ribs are tender.

Remove the ribs from the cooker and paint with Memphis-Style Championship Red Sauce. Place the ribs back on the cooker over indirect heat and cook for 20 minutes at 250°F. Remove the ribs, cut, and serve.

LEFTOVER RIB TIPS

SERVES: 4 TO 6

**COOKING METHOD:
INDIRECT HEAT**

**SUGGESTED WOOD:
HICKORY, APRICOT, PEACH,
APPLE**

**COOKING TIME:
3 HOURS 15 MINUTES**

★ ★ ★ ★ ★

10 TO 12 RIB TIPS (4 POUNDS)

DRY RUB

2 TABLESPOONS BROWN SUGAR

5½ TEASPOONS SALT

1 TABLESPOON PAPRIKA

2½ TEASPOONS BLACK PEPPER

½ TEASPOON CAYENNE PEPPER

½ TEASPOON WHITE PEPPER

SAUCE

1 CUP PREPARED BARBECUE SAUCE
(WHATEVER KIND YOU HAVE LEFT OVER)

2 TABLESPOONS RED PEPPER JELLY

2 TABLESPOONS PINEAPPLE PRESERVES

2 TABLESPOONS APRICOT PRESERVES

2 TABLESPOONS PLUM JELLY

★ ★ ★ ★ ★

When a full-size slab of spare ribs is trimmed into a St. Louis–cut spare rib, you are left with rib tips. They are found on the lower portion of the spare ribs close to the pork belly. These cut-away portions of spare ribs have small pieces of cartilage where you would expect to find bones. Rib tips are usually six inches long and one inch thick. These long strips are considered an economy cut but are surprisingly meaty.

Sometimes it seems that the best-loved barbecue specialties came into being as a way to use discarded cuts of meat, prepared with common, on-hand ingredients that are "left over." This recipe was inspired by the many hours I have stood looking into the cupboard wondering what I could make to eat. Most everyone has a cabinet full of unused spices and a refrigerator stocked with half-empty jelly jars. Fire up that old weathered bag of charcoal and enjoy!

Remove the membrane from the back of the rib tips. In a small bowl, combine the dry rub ingredients and mix well. Generously apply the rub onto the front and back sides of the ribs, patting gently to ensure that the rub adheres.

Build a fire (wood or a combination of charcoal and wood) for indirect cooking by situating the coals on only one side of the grill, leaving the other side void. If using a charcoal cooker, preheat it to 250°F. Place the rib tips meat side up on the grill, close the lid, and cook with indirect heat for 3 hours, or until the rib tips are tender.

In a small bowl, combine the sauce ingredients and mix well. Remove the rib tips from the grill and paint with the sauce. Place the rib tips back on the grill and cook over indirect heat for another 15 minutes. Remove the rib tips from the grill, cut, and serve.

DIME-AN-HOUR SPARERIBS

SERVES: 4 TO 6

COOKING METHOD:
INDIRECT HEAT

SUGGESTED WOOD:
HICKORY

COOKING TIME:
4 HOURS 20 MINUTES

★ ★ ★ ★ ★

2 SLABS PORK SPARERIBS

1 CUP WORCESTERSHIRE SAUCE

DRY RUB

2 TABLESPOONS SALT

1 TABLESPOON BLACK PEPPER

1 TABLESPOON GARLIC POWDER

MEMPHIS-STYLE CHAMPIONSHIP RED SAUCE
(PAGE 220) OR YOUR FAVORITE BRAND

★ ★ ★ ★ ★

Though the introduction of ribs to Big Bob Gibson's menu was enthusiastically embraced by the locals, the recipe itself was, well, pretty bare-bones—simply a full-size sparerib seasoned with salt and pepper and slow-smoked. In 1979, Don McLemore offered a bonus to any employee who could improve on Big Bob's ribs. During the next week the rib usage went up tenfold but profits took a nosedive, as the extremely well-fed pit workers experimented with different preparations. When the smoke cleared two weeks later, Steve Bullard earned a dime raise with this recipe.

Lay the spareribs flat in a shallow baking pan, meat side down. Pour the Worcestershire over the ribs and soak for 1 hour. In a small bowl, mix the dry rub ingredients together. Remove the ribs from the pan and coat evenly with dry rub mixture.

Build a fire (wood or a combination of charcoal and wood) for indirect cooking by situating the coals on only one side of the grill, leaving the other side void. When the cooker reaches 250°F, place the ribs meat side up on the grate and cook on a closed grill for 4 hours, or until the ribs are tender.

Paint the ribs with barbecue sauce and continue cooking meat side up for 20 minutes. Remove the ribs from the grill, cut, and serve.

★ PITMASTER'S TIP ★

On the back of all ribs is a thin membrane that lies flat against the bones. After cooking, this membrane takes on the consistency of wax paper, so you should always remove it prior to cooking.

To do this, place the slab bone side up on a cutting board. Slide your knife under the membrane and against the end bone to separate the two. With a dry paper towel or rag, grasp the edge of the thin membrane and pull. The entire membrane should separate from the rib.

There are those who argue against removing the membrane, claiming it helps hold in juices and keep the rib from drying out. The fact is most ribs contain enough fat to keep the ribs juicy with or without the membrane.

PINEAPPLE SWEET RIBS

SERVES: 4 TO 6

COOKING METHOD:
INDIRECT HEAT

SUGGESTED WOOD:
HICKORY, APPLE, PEACH

COOKING TIME:
3 HOURS 45 MINUTES

★ ★ ★ ★ ★

2 SLABS BABY BACK RIBS

DRY RUB
2 TABLESPOONS DARK BROWN SUGAR

2 TABLESPOONS PAPRIKA

1 TABLESPOON GARLIC SALT

1½ TEASPOONS ONION SALT

1½ TEASPOONS CHILI POWDER

¾ TEASPOON BLACK PEPPER

½ TEASPOON CAYENNE PEPPER

¼ TEASPOON DRIED OREGANO

¼ TEASPOON GROUND CUMIN

LIQUID SEASONING
1 CUP PINEAPPLE JUICE

1 TABLESPOON DRY RUB MIX

1½ TEASPOONS BALSAMIC VINEGAR

1½ TEASPOONS MINCED GARLIC

BIG BOB'S COMPETITION SWEET GLAZE
(PAGE 225)

★ ★ ★ ★ ★

Back ribs are sometimes referred to as loin back ribs but are most commonly called baby back ribs. The baby back rib is cut from the upper section of the rib cage below the spine and the loin muscle of the pig. A slab of baby back ribs can have as many as 15 bones (the number of bones in a pig's rib cage).

This long thin cut of pork has many defining characteristics. The bones are no thicker than a finger and are slightly curved. Because of the small bones there is generally more meat between each bone than on spare ribs. Baby back ribs are the leanest pork rib type, with a less pronounced pork flavor and a finer and denser texture.

Pineapple Sweet Ribs utilize a sweet rub and a fruity liquid seasoning, followed by a sweet glaze. The key to a multi-step rib is to layer the flavors, creating complex tastes without overpowering the pork flavor. This strategy worked at the Houston Livestock Show and Rodeo in 2004, when the judges declared this rib recipe the winner of this world championship event.

Remove the membrane from the back of the ribs. In a small bowl, combine the dry rub ingredients and mix well. Set aside 1 tablespoon of the rub for the liquid seasoning mixture and apply the remaining rub generously to the front and back sides of the ribs. Pat gently to ensure that the rub adheres to the meat.

Build a fire (wood or a combination of charcoal and wood) for indirect cooking by situating the coals on only one side of the grill, leaving the other side void. If using a charcoal cooker, preheat it to 250°F. Place the slabs meat side up on the grill, close the lid, and cook with indirect heat for 2½ hours.

Cut 2 pieces of foil large enough to wrap each slab of ribs completely and stack them to create a double layer. Remove the ribs from the grill. Place each slab meat side down on a doubled aluminum-foil square.

In a small bowl, combine the liquid seasoning ingredients, including the reserved tablespoon of dry rub seasoning. Pour ½ cup of the liquid over each slab, then tightly wrap and seal the foil. Place the wrapped slabs back in the cooker, close the lid, and cook over indirect heat for 1 hour.

Recipe continues

Remove the ribs from the cooker, unwrap, and discard the liquid and foil. Brush Big Bob's Competition Sweet Glaze on both sides of the ribs. Place the slabs in the cooker for 15 minutes, or until the sauce caramelizes. Remove the ribs from the grill, cut, and serve.

1990s

Normally in a barbecue restaurant you would think it is the pitroom workers who would appear first in the early morning. At Big Bob Gibson Bar-B-Q that is not the case; it is the pie ladies who arrive at five a.m. Some of these ladies have worked at the restaurant for as many as fifty years. You could argue it is their expertise that has kept the customers coming back to Big Bob Gibson's even more so than the barbecue.

Although fresh homemade pies have been served at Big Bob Gibson Bar-B-Q since the early 1950s, it wasn't until 1991 that wall coolers displayed the pies in the front of the restaurant. These were intentionally placed where the customers could get a quick glimpse at the slices topped with mile-high meringue. Folks might not have entered the restaurant with intentions of eating dessert, but it's hard to pass up this visual temptation. The three everyday pie offerings were lemon icebox, chocolate, and coconut cream. It was only recently that special-occasion pies, including peanut butter, banana cream, and pecan, occasionally appeared on the menu.

Thanks to a city sign ordinance the Big Bob Gibson pig no longer dances and chops with his knife, but this original marquee still stands in front of the restaurant.

Q: My pork ribs are tough! I dream of grilling ribs like my favorite barbecue stand across town, but I always have disappointing results. They taste good, but I have to gnaw them off the bone.

A: "Grilling" is the key word here. Slow it down! You may be cooking at too high a temperature. Barbecuing ribs takes between 3 and 4 hours at a temperature of 250°F. You should also make sure you are using indirect heat; ribs should not cook directly over a close heat source. If neither of these is the source of your problem, then you are simply taking the ribs off of the cooker too soon. Let them cook for an extra 30 minutes and then recheck the tenderness of the slabs.

FOUR-STAGE BARBECUE RIBS

SERVES: 4 TO 6

**COOKING METHOD:
INDIRECT HEAT**

**SUGGESTED WOOD:
HICKORY, APPLE, PECAN**

COOKING TIME: 4 HOURS

★ ★ ★ ★ ★

2 SLABS OF LOIN BACK RIBS

FIRST-STAGE DRY RUB

2 TABLESPOONS DARK BROWN SUGAR

2 TABLESPOONS PAPRIKA

1 TABLESPOON GARLIC SALT

1½ TEASPOONS ONION SALT

1½ TEASPOONS CHILI POWDER

¾ TEASPOON CAYENNE PEPPER

¾ TEASPOON BLACK PEPPER

¼ TEASPOON DRIED OREGANO

¼ TEASPOON WHITE PEPPER

¼ TEASPOON GROUND CUMIN

SECOND-STAGE LIQUID SEASONING

¾ CUP GRAPE JUICE

¾ CUP APPLE JUICE

THIRD-STAGE DRY RUB

2 TABLESPOONS FIRST-STAGE RUB

1 TABLESPOON BROWN SUGAR

FINISHING GLAZE

¾ CUP BIG BOB GIBSON CHAMPIONSHIP RED SAUCE (AVAILABLE AT RETAIL OUTLETS) OR YOUR FAVORITE BOTTLED BRAND

¼ CUP HONEY

In 2001, I made my first national television appearance on Food Network's **Cooking Live with Sara Moulton**. I received the invitation after doing a morning radio show with Sara at the Memphis in May World Championship Barbecue Cooking Contest. Her only stipulation was that my recipes needed to be cooked in an indoor oven. I have always maintained that any recipe written for the kitchen can be duplicated outdoors with more flavor; here my challenge was to prove the opposite holds true as well. I developed a four-stage rib recipe that layers flavors to make up for the extra punch you can only get from cooking with burning coals. It was pretty successful, but changing the recipe back to the outdoor cooker gives these ribs the best of both worlds.

Remove the membrane from the back of the ribs. In a small bowl, combine the first-stage dry rub ingredients and mix well. Set aside 2 tablespoons of this rub mix for the third-stage dry rub and generously apply the remaining rub to the front and back sides of the ribs. Pat gently to ensure the rub adheres.

Build a fire (wood or a combination of charcoal and wood) for indirect cooking by situating the coals on only one side of the grill, leaving the other side void. If using a charcoal cooker, pre-heat it to 250°F. Place the slabs meat side up on the grill, close the lid, and cook with indirect heat for 2 hours and 15 minutes.

Cut 2 pieces of aluminum foil large enough to wrap each slab of ribs completely and stack them to create a double layer. Remove the ribs from the grill. Place each slab meat side down on a doubled aluminum-foil square. In a small bowl, stir together the liquid seasoning ingredients and pour ¾ cup over each slab. Wrap and seal each slab tightly in the foil. Place the wrapped slabs back in the cooker, close the lid, and cook over indirect heat for 1 hour.

In another small bowl, combine the reserved first-stage dry rub with the brown sugar to make the third-stage rub. Remove the wrapped ribs from the cooker. Discard the liquid and foil and apply a light coat of the third-stage rub to the meat side of the ribs. Return the ribs to the cooker, meat side up, and cook uncov-ered for 30 minutes. Mix the finishing glaze ingredients and brush the glaze on both sides of the ribs. Continue cooking for 10 to 15 minutes, or until the sauce caramelizes. Remove the ribs from the grill, cut, and serve.

BRAISED BARBECUE BEEF BACK RIBS

SERVES: 6

COOKING METHOD:
INDIRECT HEAT

SUGGESTED WOOD:
HICKORY, OAK, MESQUITE

MARINATING TIME:
45 MINUTES

COOKING TIME:
4 HOURS 15 MINUTES

★ ★ ★ ★ ★

2 SLABS BEEF BACK RIBS

DRY RUB

1½ TABLESPOONS GRANULATED SUGAR

1½ TABLESPOONS BROWN SUGAR

1½ TABLESPOONS KOSHER SALT

1½ TABLESPOONS PAPRIKA

¾ TEASPOON BLACK PEPPER

¼ TEASPOON CAYENNE PEPPER

SOY MARINADE (PAGE 237)

BRAISING LIQUID

1 CUP BEEF BROTH

2 TABLESPOONS WORCESTERSHIRE SAUCE

★ ★ ★ ★ ★

Because of the slab size and the large bones, beef back ribs are sometimes referred to as "dinosaur ribs." Back ribs are one of the least expensive cuts of beef. They are prized in the South as comfort food, though they are rarely seen in other parts of the country.

If beef ribs are grilled hot and fast they will toughen up and require a good set of choppers to gnaw them off the bone. Braising is the most popular method to tenderize beef ribs.

I cook my beef back ribs at a low temperature in a small amount of liquid for a long period of time. This cooking method produces very tender and juicy results, but without the crusty exterior of a grilled rib. While they can be browned on the stovetop over high heat, I brown the ribs in the outdoor cooker to heighten the barbecue flavor. This method approximates the effect of braising on the grill.

Remove the membrane from the back of the ribs. In a small bowl, add the dry rub ingredients, mix well, and set aside. Put the soy marinade in a resealable plastic bag or a shallow dish. Marinate the beef back ribs for 45 minutes in the soy marinade.

Build a fire (wood or a combination of charcoal and wood) for indirect cooking by situating the coals on only one side of the grill, leaving the other side void. Remove the ribs from the marinade, pat dry, and apply an even coat of the dry rub to all sides. Place the beef ribs on the cooker (bone side down) away from the coals, close the lid, and cook with indirect heat (approximately 250°F) for 2 hours.

Remove the ribs from the grill and place them in the center of a doubled sheet of aluminum foil, meat side facing down. In a small bowl, combine the beef broth and Worcestershire to make the braising liquid. Pour the braising liquid over the ribs and wrap tightly in the foil to trap the juices inside. Return the foil pack to the grill, close the lid, and cook for 2 hours and 15 minutes, or until tender.

Let the beef rest in the foil for 15 minutes before serving.

COUNTRY-STYLE RIBS
with Apple Bourbon Barbecue Sauce

SERVES: 6

COOKING METHOD:
INDIRECT HEAT

SUGGESTED WOOD:
HICKORY, APPLE, MAPLE

COOKING TIME:
3 HOURS 20 MINUTES

★ ★ ★ ★ ★

DRY RUB

¼ CUP BROWN SUGAR

6½ TEASPOONS SALT

2 TABLESPOONS PAPRIKA

1½ TEASPOONS GARLIC POWDER

1½ TEASPOONS GROUND CUMIN

1½ TEASPOONS ONION POWDER

1 TEASPOON BLACK PEPPER

¼ TEASPOON GROUND CINNAMON

¼ TEASPOON GROUND GINGER

12 COUNTRY-STYLE RIBS

APPLE BOURBON BARBECUE SAUCE
(PAGE 227)

★ ★ ★ ★ ★

Because of their varying sizes and meat types, cook times on country-style ribs are a little difficult to pinpoint. True country-style ribs are very thick and can take up to an extra hour of cook time compared to the ones labeled "shoulder-cut country-style ribs." If your ribs have a large cross-section of loin meat (light pink color), your cook time should be less or the lean loin meat will dry out. Your best gauge of doneness is a simple squeeze with your fingertips. If the meat feels rubbery, it needs more cooking. The meat from a perfectly cooked rib can be easily pinched from the bone.

Over the years I have found that country-style ribs are an extremely versatile cut. They can be grilled hot or barbecued low and slow, and they partner well with dry rubs or marinades, sweet or savory. This recipe utilizes both a dry rub and a sweet sauce to highlight the flavor of the tender meat achieved by low-heat indirect cooking. One more word of advice: Don't be bashful when applying the sauce. Slop it on!

In a small bowl, combine the dry rub ingredients and mix well. Apply generously to the front and back sides of the ribs, patting gently to ensure it will adhere.

Build a fire (wood or a combination of charcoal and wood) for indirect cooking by situating the coals on only one side of the grill, leaving the other side void. If using a charcoal cooker, preheat it to 250°F. Place the ribs meat side up on the grill, close the lid, and cook with indirect heat for 3 hours, or until the ribs are tender.

Remove the ribs from the cooker and paint with the sauce. Place the ribs back on the cooker, close the lid, and cook over indirect heat for 20 minutes at 250°F. Remove the ribs and serve.

⋆ PITMASTER'S TIP ⋆

During the barbecue process some meat develops a pink ring around its outer edges. This "smoke ring" can sometimes be mistaken for undercooked meat, but it is a natural result of cooking low and slow. This pink tint is not a result of smoke penetrating and coloring the muscle; instead, it is the result of a chemical reaction between nitrogen dioxide and the meat's pigment.

Some view a deep smoke ring as a badge of honor reflecting their cooking skill. I am not one of these people because I have tasted flavorful 'Q without a smoke ring and bland 'Q with a large pink band. There are several ways you can enhance the color and depth of a smoke ring:

- Meat with a moist surface absorbs nitrogen dioxide more readily. Ensure that the meat stays moist as it cooks by placing a water pan inside the cooker and keeping the cooker's lid closed.
- Use wet or fresh-cut (green) wood, providing a moist heat to your cooker.
- Cook the meat slowly to give the gas more time to react with the pigment.
- More nitrogen dioxide is produced with burning flames than with smoldering fires, so cook the meat with a hot fire using an indirect cooking method.
- Prior to cooking, season the meat with a curing agent containing sodium nitrate.

BARBECUE BEEF SHORT RIBS

SERVES: 5

COOKING METHOD:
INDIRECT HEAT

SUGGESTED WOOD:
HICKORY, OAK, MESQUITE

COOKING TIME:
2 HOURS 30 MINUTES

★ ★ ★ ★ ★

10 BEEF SHORT RIBS CUT INTO
INDIVIDUAL RIBS

DRY RUB

1 TABLESPOON SALT

4 TEASPOONS BLACK PEPPER

2 TEASPOONS DARK BROWN SUGAR

2 TEASPOONS DRIED OREGANO

2 TEASPOONS GARLIC POWDER

1½ TEASPOONS DRIED THYME

1 TEASPOON GROUND GINGER

STOCK

1 CUP BEEF BROTH

3 TABLESPOONS SOY SAUCE

4 TEASPOONS MINCED SHALLOTS

2 TEASPOONS WORCESTERSHIRE SAUCE

★ ★ ★ ★ ★

A full slab of beef short ribs usually contains 3 to 4 bones and is typically 8 to 10 inches square. The thickness will vary depending on the butcher but ranges from 2 to 5 inches. There are several ways beef ribs are cut and presented to the consumer besides the full slab. The ribs can be individually cut with a size similar to a pork country-style rib, cross-cut across the bones about ½ inch thick, or cut into boneless steaks.

Beef ribs are less common to my barbecue region than pork ribs. I always look forward to working with cuts of meat that aren't on the Big Bob Gibson menu. This recipe is one I created while working for the Kingsford charcoal company in 2007. I love the intense beefy flavor of the seasoned juices that result from this preparation; the juices can be drizzled back over the beef ribs or used to flavor a side dish such as mashed potatoes.

Remove the membrane from the back of the ribs. With a sharp knife, score the top of each rib by cutting ¼-inch grooves perpendicular to the rib bone every ½ inch. These cuts will provide more surface area of bark (the flavorful crust).

In a small bowl, combine the dry rub ingredients and mix well. Apply a generous coat of the rub to all sides of each rib.

Build a fire (wood or a combination of charcoal and wood) for indirect cooking by situating the coals on only one side of the grill, leaving the other side void. Place the beef ribs on the cooker (bone side down) away from the coals, close the lid, and cook with indirect heat (approximately 275°F) for 1½ hours or until the internal temperature of the beef is 160°F.

Remove the ribs from the grill and place them in the center of a doubled sheet of aluminum foil, meat side down. In a small bowl, combine the stock mixture and pour it over the ribs. Wrap tightly in foil, trapping the juice inside. Return the foil pack to the grill, close the lid, and cook over indirect heat for 1 hour, or until the internal temperature of the beef reaches 200°F.

Remove the foil packet from the grill and let the beef rest in the foil for 15 minutes. Unwrap the ribs and slice each one to the bone at all of the scored cuts. This will create bite-size chunks of meat and allow the juice to penetrate the bark, providing more flavor.

RACK OF LAMB
with Mixed Herb Seasoning

SERVES: 4 TO 6

COOKING METHOD:
INDIRECT AND DIRECT HEAT

SUGGESTED WOOD:
HICKORY, OAK, PECAN

COOKING TIME:
36 MINUTES

★ ★ ★ ★ ★

2 RACKS OF LAMB

SEASONING PASTE

¾ TEASPOON DRIED ROSEMARY

¾ TEASPOON DRIED THYME

¾ TEASPOON DRIED OREGANO

4½ TEASPOONS SALT

3 TEASPOONS PAPRIKA

2 TEASPOONS BLACK PEPPER

2 TEASPOONS GARLIC POWDER

¾ TEASPOON GROUND GINGER

2 TABLESPOONS EXTRA-VIRGIN OLIVE OIL

1½ TEASPOONS SOY SAUCE

KOSHER SALT
BLACK PEPPER

★ ★ ★ ★ ★

Rack of lamb is the rib section of the lamb, extending from the shoulder to the loin. The majority of lamb is graded as choice or prime, so it is not difficult to find a good-quality rack. Lamb is available at most quality butcher houses or grocery stores. When selecting a rack of lamb, make sure that the backbone, or chine, has been removed. This will make slicing each lamb chop easier, prior to serving.

If you've shied away from serving lamb to your picky eaters, give this recipe a spin; it is one of my family's favorites. Keep in mind that my kids are just as picky eaters as yours. Rack of lamb is the best way to introduce children to the distinct deep flavor of lamb meat, the only downside being the relatively high price per pound. There is something about "lamb on a stick" that appeals to the young ones. In the end, though, it is the flavor of this recipe that will have the kids requesting second helpings.

Start out by frenching each rack of lamb (see Pitmaster's Tip). Cover the exposed bones by wrapping them individually in aluminum foil. This will prevent them from burning during the cooking process.

Lightly chop the dried rosemary. Scrape the dried rosemary into a small bowl and add the remaining seasoning paste ingredients. Mix well until a paste forms. Apply the paste evenly to each lamb rack.

Build a charcoal and/or wood fire on one side of the grill, leaving the other side void. This will create two zones for cooking, indirect and direct. Preheat to 450°F.

Place the lamb directly over the heat and cook for 5 to 6 minutes on each side. When the rack is well browned, move it to the area of indirect heat. Close the grill lid and cook for an additional 12 minutes on each side over indirect heat. Remove the lamb when the internal temperature reaches 125°F for rare or 135°F for medium rare.

Let the lamb rest under tented foil on a cutting board for 10 to 15 minutes, then use a sharp knife to cut between each bone, separating into individual lamb chops. Lightly season the cut sides of each chop with kosher salt and black pepper. Return the chops to the grill over direct heat for 30 seconds on each side. Remove from the grill and serve immediately.

★ PITMASTER'S TIP ★

Trimming a rack of lamb to expose the rib bones makes a beautiful presentation. The process is called frenching. To french lamb ribs, place the rack, bone side down, on a cutting board. With a sharp knife make a cut perpendicular to the bones through the fat layer, where the bones adjoin the meat. When the knife touches the bones, angle it away from the eye meat and cut toward the end of the bones. Cut the meat from in between the bones, using a small knife. Use the point of the knife to scrape the fat and bits of meat from the bones. The bones should be smooth and clean when finished.

RED-SKIN POTATO SALAD

SERVES: 12

COOKING METHOD: **STOVE**

COOKING TIME: **15 MINUTES**

★ ★ ★ ★ ★

6 CUPS UNPEELED DICED RED-SKIN POTATOES

4 HARD-BOILED EGGS, CHOPPED WELL

¾ CUP MAYONNAISE

⅓ CUP SWEET PICKLE RELISH

¼ CUP WHITE ONION, CHOPPED FINE

1½ TEASPOONS SALT

½ TEASPOON BLACK PEPPER

⅛ TEASPOON CELERY SEED

★ ★ ★ ★ ★

Traditional Southern potato salads are usually served chilled and contain either a mustard- or mayonnaise-based dressing. Big Bob Gibson Bar-B-Q first served a mustard-based potato salad, but over the years the recipe has gradually changed to a mayonnaise version. Because of the high ratio of hard-boiled eggs, it can almost be classified as a potato and egg salad.

Place the diced potatoes in a large pot and cover with water. Boil the potatoes, uncovered, until tender, 12 to 15 minutes. Drain and transfer the potatoes to a mixing bowl. Add the remaining ingredients, and mix gently with a rubber spatula. Chill and serve.

BLACK-EYED PEAS WITH HOG JOWL
with Caramelized Sweet Onions and Collard Greens

Superstition across the southeastern United States holds that eating hog jowls, collard greens, and black-eyed peas on New Year's Day will make a person healthy, wealthy, and wise. Hog jowl, which is the cheek of a pig, is a flavorful and fatty meat that is usually cured or smoked. Hard to believe a food as rich and fat-laden as hog jowl is linked to health and prosperity. These meager foods have always been a symbol of plenty for people who are often very poor.

SERVES: 12

COOKING METHOD: STOVE

COOKING TIME: 2 HOURS

★ ★ ★ ★ ★

9 CUPS WATER

8 OUNCES HOG JOWL OR HAM HOCK (PREFERABLY SMOKED)

1 POUND DRIED BLACK-EYED PEAS, CLEANED AND RINSED

10 OUNCES COLLARD GREENS (TWO BUNCHES), STEMS REMOVED, RINSED

1 SWEET ONION

3 TABLESPOONS BUTTER

2 GARLIC CLOVES, MINCED

¼ CUP TOMATO SAUCE

1½ TABLESPOONS WHITE DISTILLED VINEGAR

1½ TABLESPOONS SUGAR

1½ TABLESPOONS SALT

¾ TEASPOON BLACK PEPPER

½ TEASPOON HOT SAUCE

JUST ADD GREENS PEPPER SAUCE (PAGE 234)

★ ★ ★ ★ ★

The "good-luck" traditions of black-eyed peas in the Southern United States date back to the Civil War, when Union troops ravaged Southern lands, destroying crops and taking all livestock. All that was left were black-eyed peas, which were considered to be fodder for horses and other animals; as a result, many Southerners subsisted on this protein-rich and hearty legume.

In a large saucepan combine the water and the hog jowl or ham hock. Cook at a boil for 1 hour and 15 minutes. Use tongs to remove the pork from the pot and when cool enough to handle, separate the meat from the fat, skin, and bones. Dice the meat and return it to the pot with the stock and set aside.

Place the peas in a medium-size saucepan and cover with cold water. Bring to a rolling boil, then immediately remove from the heat, cover, and let stand for 1 hour.

Stack the clean collard green leaves and cut into 1- to 2-inch squares.

Peel and halve the onion and cut in ¼-inch slices. Separate the onion into strips. In a large nonstick skillet, cook the onions over medium heat for 5 minutes without stirring. Add the butter, garlic, and collard greens to the skillet and stir well. Cover and cook for an additional 5 minutes, stirring occasionally.

Drain the beans and add them to the pot with the pork stock along with the onions and collards. Add the remaining ingredients and stir well. Cover, bring to a boil over high heat, then turn to low and simmer for 45 minutes, stirring occasionally until vegetables soften.

Top each serving with a few dashes of Just Add Greens Pepper Sauce or pass the sauce at the table.

MIXED VEGETABLE GRILL
with Balsamic-Honey Marinade

SERVES: 8

COOKING METHOD:
DIRECT HEAT

MARINATING TIME:
2 TO 3 HOURS

COOKING TIME:
6 TO 10 MINUTES

★ ★ ★ ★ ★

2 YELLOW SUMMER SQUASH

2 GREEN ZUCCHINI

1 EGGPLANT

1 RED BELL PEPPER

1 GREEN BELL PEPPER

1 YELLOW BELL PEPPER

1 RED ONION

4 ROMA TOMATOES

1 POUND BUTTON MUSHROOMS

MARINADE

¾ CUP BALSAMIC VINEGAR

¾ CUP VEGETABLE OIL

¾ CUP HONEY

1 TABLESPOON SALT

2 TEASPOONS BLACK PEPPER

3 TABLESPOONS CHOPPED FRESH FLAT-LEAF
PARSLEY LEAVES

★ ★ ★ ★ ★

The perfect complement to all types of barbecued ribs is a large bowl of mixed grilled vegetables. The charred highlights of the multicolored dish make it as appealing to look at as it is to eat. Oil makes the colors of the vegetables glisten, while the balsamic vinegar and honey provide a rich, sweet flavor.

Quarter the squash, zucchini, and eggplant lengthwise and cut in half. Quarter the peppers and discard the cores and seeds. Cut the onion into thick slices. Cut the tomatoes in half. Place the vegetables in a large bowl along with the mushrooms.

In a small bowl, combine the marinade ingredients and mix well. Pour the marinade over the vegetables, cover, and chill for 2 to 3 hours.

Build a charcoal and/or wood fire for direct grilling. Remove the vegetables from the marinade and place in a grill basket directly over the coals (approximately 450°F) for 3 to 5 minutes on each side. Transfer the vegetables to a large serving bowl. Add the parsley, mix well, and serve.

CARAMEL PECAN MINI-PIES

COOKING METHOD: OVEN

COOKING TIME: 20 MINUTES

SERVES: 6

★ ★ ★ ★ ★

1 PACKAGE PHYLLO DOUGH, DEFROSTED IF FROZEN

6 STORE-BOUGHT CARAMELS, WRAPPERS REMOVED

½ CUP PECAN PIECES

¼ CUP DARK CORN SYRUP

½ CUP SUGAR

1½ TABLESPOONS BUTTER

½ TEASPOON PURE VANILLA EXTRACT

⅛ TEASPOON SALT

1 TABLESPOON WATER

1 EGG, LIGHTLY BEATEN

★ ★ ★ ★ ★

This is a traditional Southern holiday dessert, though the mysteries of its origins have been lost to time. Having had some less-than-wonderful renditions in my time, I decided to come up with my own ideal version. I went to the test kitchen with two things in mind: First, too much corn syrup yields a pie that is too sweet and runny. There is nothing worse than a pie with a soggy crust and syrup pooling in the pan where a piece has been cut out. Second, beating the eggs too much destroys the creamy texture of a properly cooked pecan pie. I am pretty pleased with these results, and I bet you will be too.

Preheat the oven to 300°F.

Stack 6 sheets of phyllo dough on a work surface. Using a 4-inch cookie cutter, cut 6 circles, each containing the 6 sheets of phyllo.

Spray a 6-cup muffin pan with nonstick spray. Place 1 layered circle of phyllo into each cup. Place 1 caramel and 1½ tablespoons of pecans into each cup.

Heat the corn syrup, sugar, butter, vanilla extract, salt, and water in a small saucepan until the ingredients are combined. Stir in the egg. Divide the mixture among the 6 pastry cups.

Bake for 20 minutes, or until the pies turn a rich brown and are firm in the center. Cool in the muffin pan for 15 minutes before removing and serving.

CHAPTER 7

SAUCES AND SLATHERS

★ ★ ★ ★ ★

THE BIGGEST MISCONCEPTION ABOUT BARBECUE IS

that "the sauce is the boss." Many people believe that a rich tomato-based barbecue sauce will turn any pile of meat into delicious barbecue. This is far from the truth. The real secret of barbecue is the flavor derived from the process, not the sauce.

This is not to minimize the key role sauce can play in a good plate of barbecue. Sauce helps define your personal style as well as that of the major barbecue regions in this country. Four distinct barbecue regions are historically recognized: the Carolinas, Memphis, Texas, and Kansas City. Each region is defined by a preferred meat, type of wood, and type of sauce (see chart). Although classifying barbecue into four regions is neat and tidy, it inadequately describes barbecue in America. Where each of the major regions overlap, there are sub-regions of barbecue, many of which have similar characteristics but are noted for their own specialties (example: Kentucky Mutton). In North Alabama, we are caught between the vinegar sauces and pork shoulders of the Carolinas and the sweet sauce of Memphis, and over the years we have been influenced by both regions. Big Bob Gibson Bar-B-Q's solution is to serve our pulled pork right off the pit and offer various table sauces to suit our customers' demands.

★ ★ ★ ★ ★

REGION	PREFERRED MEAT	TYPE OF WOOD	TYPE OF SAUCE
CAROLINAS	WHOLE HOG PORK SHOULDER	HICKORY OAK	RANGES FROM VINEGAR TO VINEGAR-KETCHUP–BASED TO MUSTARD-BASED
MEMPHIS	PORK RIBS PORK BUTT/SHOULDER	HICKORY	TOMATO-BASED SWEET/TANGY
TEXAS	BEEF BRISKET PORK AND BEEF RIBS SAUSAGE	MESQUITE OAK	RANGES FROM SPICY TOMATO TO SAUCELESS
KANSAS CITY	BEEF BRISKET PORK BUTT PORK RIBS	OAK HICKORY	TOMATO BASED (THICK) SWEET/SPICY
NORTH ALABAMA	PORK SHOULDER WHOLE CHICKENS	HICKORY	RANGES FROM VINEGAR TO SWEET TOMATO-BASED TO MAYONNAISE-BASED

When Big Bob Gibson began serving his barbecue in 1925, he used only two sauces. His pork was doused with a simple thin vinegar sop mop during the cooking process, and more of the sauce was offered on the side if his customers chose to season their meat with a little more of the tangy liquid. Every chicken that came out of his pit was submerged in a vat of white barbecue sauce, and there was always a bottle of the white sauce at the table for those who wanted a little extra. This white sauce is unique to our region of the country and is a defining attribute of North Alabama barbecue to this day.

For many years the roster of sauces at Big Bob Gibson's remained unchanged. But in 1996, we learned the value of a good barbecue sauce firsthand when we started to compete in barbecue cooking competitions. That was the year we acquired a large trailer with two huge barbecue cookers, intending to use this portable cooking rig to pick up more catering jobs. As an afterthought we entered a barbecue cooking contest to promote Big Bob Gibson catering with our newest acquisition. With a fourth-place finish we learned two things: Not everyone is familiar with barbecue white sauce, and judges appreciate a sauce to accompany their barbecue!

That was the inspiration my father-in-law, Don McLemore, and I needed to try our hands at a sweet tomato-based sauce. After long hours in the kitchen, Don sent me a sample along with the recipe. I would taste his, make a few adjustments that I felt had bettered his attempt, then send him a revised recipe with a sauce sample. This process of trading sauces back and forth went on for a year until it was time to go to our first Memphis in May World Barbecue Championship. Unable to decide which sauce to use (not surprisingly, he liked his and I liked mine), we mixed equal parts of the sauces and the resulting super sauce won the sauce competition.

With our first blue ribbon in competition coming from the Memphis in May contest, we were inspired to stay in the kitchen and experiment with dry rubs, injections, and, of course, more sauces. The resulting fruits of our labor encompass not only sauces but mops, sops, and rubs, all guaranteed to elevate your barbecue to a world-championship level.

PRESENT DAY

If only the walls could talk at Big Bob Gibson Bar-B-Q. The stories of Big Bob told over and over again have turned him into a legend within these walls, even more so than our customers view him. The generations that followed him and preceded me—Coy and Punk McLemore, Don and Carolyn McLemore—have built upon the foundation he started and helped turn this sleepy little mom-and-pop restaurant into a barbecue mecca.

Big Bob Gibson Bar-B-Q is now known throughout the world as a destination for great barbecue. Our barbecue seasoning and sauces, including Big Bob's original-recipe white sauce, can be found at grocery stores across the Southeast. Our first franchise opened in Monroe, North Carolina, in 2007. And as an ultimate feather in our cap, the Big Bob Gibson Bar-B-Q Competition Cooking Team has won ten world barbecue championships. A lot has been accomplished, but there is much more to do before the fifth generation takes over.

1990s AND 2000s

In recent years, barbecue cooking competitions have become a favorite weekend activity for many barbecue enthusiasts. The popularity of these events has grown to such an extreme that most weekends there are about a dozen competitions to choose from. For several years the Big Bob Gibson Competition Cooking Team cooked all over the country, competing head-to-head against as many as five hundred teams. Although we don't cook in as many contests as we once did, the Big Bob Gibson team's skills and a few new techniques have proved to be a winning combination. Here's a list of some of our awards.

MEMPHIS IN MAY WORLD CHAMPIONSHIP BARBECUE COOKING CONTEST

1997	1st place Barbecue Sauce
1999	1st place Barbecue Sauce
	1st place Pork
2000	1st place Pork—Grand Champion
2001	1st place Pork
2002	1st place Pork
2003	1st place Pork—Grand Champion
2004	1st place Pork

AMERICAN ROYAL BARBECUE, INTERNATIONAL INVITATIONAL AND BARBECUE SAUCE CONTEST

1995	1st place White Barbecue Sauce
1998	1st place Barbecue Sauce
	"Best Sauce on the Planet"
2002	1st place Chicken
	Open Reserve Grand Champion
2004	1st place Brisket
	Invitational Grand Champion
2007	1st place Pork

INTERNATIONAL JAMAICAN JERK STYLE/SOUTHERN BARBECUE COOK-OFF

2003	Grand Champion

HOUSTON LIVESTOCK SHOW AND RODEO WORLD'S CHAMPIONSHIP BAR-B-Q CONTEST

2004	1st place Ribs
	Reserve Grand Champion

ALABAMA STATE BARBECUE CHAMPIONSHIP

1999	1st place Pork—Grand Champion
2000	1st place Pork
	1st place Ribs—Grand Champion
2001	1st place Pork—Grand Champion

TENNESSEE STATE BARBECUE CHAMPIONSHIP

1998	1st place Pork—Grand Champion
1999	1st place Pork—Grand Champion
2000	1st place Pork—Grand Champion
2001	1st place Pork—Grand Champion

WASHINGTON STATE BARBECUE CHAMPIONSHIP

2004	1st place Pork
	1st place Ribs

CHILE PEPPER MAGAZINE BARBECUE AWARDS

2000	1st place Barbecue Sauce
2001	1st place Vinegar Barbecue Sauce
	1st place Mustard Barbecue Sauce
2002	1st place Spicy Mustard Barbecue Sauce
2003	1st place Mustard Barbecue Sauce
2004	1st place Mustard Barbecue Sauce
2005	1st place Mustard Barbecue Sauce
2006	1st place Seasoning and Dry Rub
2008	1st place Seasoning and Dry Rub
	1st place Barbecue Sauce

NATIONAL BARBECUE ASSOCIATION AWARDS OF EXCELLENCE

2000   "Restaurant of the Year"
        1st place Hot Barbecue Sauce
        1st place Vinegar Barbecue Sauce
        1st place Mustard Barbecue Sauce

2001   1st place Vinegar Barbecue Sauce

2002   1st place Mustard Barbecue Sauce

2003   1st place Mild Vinegar Barbecue Sauce
        1st place Hot Vinegar Barbecue Sauce
        1st place Mustard Barbecue Sauce
        1st place Hot Barbecue Sauce

2004   1st place Barbecue Sauce
        1st place Hot Barbecue Sauce
        1st place Mild Vinegar Sauce

2005   1st place Hot Barbecue Sauce

2007   1st place Mustard Barbecue Sauce
        1st place Hot Barbecue Sauce

2008   1st place Hot Barbecue Sauce

SCOVIE AWARDS

2007   1st place Seasoning and Dry Rub

2008   1st place Mustard Sauce

2008   1st place Barbecue Sauce

THE SOUTHERN PRIDE CUP, WORLD CUP

2001   1st place

2002   1st place
        Grand Champion

TEXAS FIERY FOOD CHALLENGE

2001   1st place Barbecue Sauce

2002   1st place Hot Barbecue Sauce

LOUISIANA STATE BARBECUE CHAMPIONSHIP

1999   1st place Beef
        Grand Champion

AMERICAN INSTITUTE OF WINE AND FOOD BBQ RIB FLY-IN

2003   1st place, "Best Ribs in America"

2004   1st place, "Best Ribs in America"

JACK DANIEL'S WORLD CHAMPIONSHIP INVITATIONAL BARBECUE

2003   1st place Pork

"DON'T AIM FOR SUCCESS IF YOU WANT IT; JUST DO WHAT YOU LOVE AND BELIEVE IN, AND IT WILL COME NATURALLY."

DAVID FROST

Overleaf: Many World Championship trophies are on display at Big Bob Gibson Bar-B-Q, along with plenty of magazine and newspaper articles for customers to read while they wait for a table.

BIG BOB GIBSON BAR-B-Q WHITE SAUCE

MAKES: 4 CUPS

★　★　★　★　★

2 CUPS MAYONNAISE

1 CUP DISTILLED WHITE VINEGAR

½ CUP APPLE JUICE

2 TEASPOONS PREPARED HORSERADISH

2 TEASPOONS GROUND BLACK PEPPER

2 TEASPOONS FRESH LEMON JUICE

1 TEASPOON SALT

½ TEASPOON CAYENNE PEPPER

★　★　★　★　★

People raised in Decatur, Alabama, know that barbecue sauce is supposed to be white. For more than eighty years Big Bob Gibson's has been dunking its golden-brown birds, fifty at a time, into a vat of this tangy, peppery white sauce. The steaming, glistening chickens are then cut to order for our customers.

For years and years the restaurant's early-morning cooks closely guarded the white sauce recipe, which was made each day before the day shift arrived. However, even without doing the math, I can tell you that hundreds of cooks have passed through the pit-rooms of Big Bob Gibson Bar-B-Q, so I don't think you can describe this recipe as "closely guarded" anymore.

I do know that Big Bob's techniques and recipes, including his white sauce, have influenced the flavors of regional barbecue in Alabama. The great thing about passing secrets is that every time they are shared they change slightly. There is now a large number of "authentic" versions of Big Bob's original secret recipe and cooking method—all different from one another. This is one of my favorite examples.

In a large bowl, combine all the ingredients and blend well. Use as a marinade, baste, or dipping sauce. Store refrigerated in an airtight container for up to 2 weeks.

MEMPHIS-STYLE CHAMPIONSHIP RED SAUCE

MAKES: 4 CUPS

COOKING METHOD: STOVE

COOKING TIME:
10 TO 15 MINUTES

★ ★ ★ ★ ★

1¼ CUPS KETCHUP

1 CUP WATER

¾ CUP VINEGAR

¾ CUP TOMATO PASTE

¾ CUP BROWN SUGAR

⅔ CUP CORN SYRUP

½ CUP PURE MAPLE SYRUP

4 TABLESPOONS HONEY

3 TABLESPOONS MOLASSES

4 TEASPOONS SALT

4 TEASPOONS WORCESTERSHIRE SAUCE

1 TABLESPOON APPLESAUCE

1½ TEASPOONS SOY SAUCE

1½ TEASPOONS LIQUID SMOKE

1 TEASPOON ONION POWDER

¾ TEASPOON CORNSTARCH

½ TEASPOON DRIED MUSTARD POWDER

½ TEASPOON CAYENNE PEPPER

¼ TEASPOON BLACK PEPPER

⅛ TEASPOON GARLIC POWDER

⅛ TEASPOON WHITE PEPPER

⅛ TEASPOON CELERY SEED

⅛ TEASPOON GROUND CUMIN

★ ★ ★ ★ ★

Memphis-Style Championship Red Sauce is very similar to our award-winning Big Bob Gibson Championship Red Sauce, which is available at retail outlets, with one key difference: In competition I often add extra sweetener to the sauce to give our barbecue a glossy, sweet glaze. If you prefer a less sweet sauce, reduce the honey and molasses by two tablespoons each.

Combine all the sauce ingredients in a medium nonreative saucepan and blend well. Bring to a boil, then reduce the heat and simmer over medium-low heat for 10 to 15 minutes. Allow the sauce to cool, then transfer to a tightly covered jar or plastic container. Store refrigerated for up to 2 weeks.

EASTERN CAROLINA PIG PICKIN' SAUCE

MAKES: 6½ CUPS

★ ★ ★ ★ ★

5 CUPS DISTILLED VINEGAR

1 CUP CIDER VINEGAR

5 TABLESPOONS DARK BROWN SUGAR

3 TABLESPOONS SALT

1½ TABLESPOONS CAYENNE PEPPER

1 TABLESPOON HOT SAUCE

2 TEASPOONS CRUSHED RED PEPPER FLAKES

1 TEASPOON BLACK PEPPER

★ ★ ★ ★ ★

I think it's safe to assume that the history of barbecue in North Carolina traveled from east to west. If you have any doubt, you only need to look at the ingredient difference between the two styles of sauce. In the East a barbecue sauce can be as simple as vinegar, salt, and pepper. Western North Carolina compounds the East's flavors with a variety of extra ingredients including ketchup, a generous amount of brown sugar, and sometimes Worcestershire sauce (See page 224).

Eastern Carolina barbecue has generally consisted of cooking whole hogs, but it is the vinegar sauce that adds an element of uniqueness to its barbecue. The sauce will add an increased level of moisture to the chopped meat while enhancing its flavor with a distinct cider-vinegar tang.

Combine the ingredients in a large nonreative bowl and mix well. Make at least 24 hours prior to usage for best flavor. Store the sauce in a tightly covered jar for up to 2 months refrigerated.

BIG BOB GIBSON BAR-B-Q VINEGAR SOP MOP

MAKES: 7 CUPS

★ ★ ★ ★ ★

6½ CUPS DISTILLED COLORED VINEGAR
(SUBSTITUTE WHITE VINEGAR)

½ CUP CAYENNE PEPPER

2 TABLESPOONS SALT

3 SLICES LEMON

★ ★ ★ ★ ★

To barbecue aficionados it is clear that Big Bob Gibson was directly influenced by the conventions of Eastern North Carolina–style barbecue. The connection can't be made through the family tree, but the ingredients in his vinegar-based sop make it obvious. The only difference is that Big Bob didn't share North Carolinians' affinity for apple cider vinegar, preferring distilled colored vinegar instead.

This straightforward concoction has been mopped onto the restaurant's pork shoulders since the very beginning. I am pleased to reveal that this four-ingredient "secret sauce" is Big Bob's original recipe; maybe now the sauce bottles on the restaurant tables will stop disappearing.

In a large bowl, combine the ingredients and mix well. Make at least 24 hours prior to usage for best flavor. Store the sauce in a tightly covered jar for up to 2 weeks at room temperature.

WESTERN CAROLINA PIG DIP

MAKES: 6½ CUPS

★ ★ ★ ★ ★

4 CUPS DISTILLED VINEGAR

2 CUPS KETCHUP

½ CUP BROWN SUGAR

8 TEASPOONS WORCESTERSHIRE SAUCE

4 TEASPOONS SALT

1 TABLESPOON PAPRIKA

1 TEASPOON HOT SAUCE

1 TEASPOON BLACK PEPPER

★ ★ ★ ★ ★

Raleigh, the capital of North Carolina, serves as the state's east-west dividing point in Carolina barbecue. To the east of the city, whole hog is the meat of choice and simple Eastern Carolina-style vinegar sauce is the preferred slather. West of Raleigh is the land of the pork shoulder, and the "sauce" is referred to as a "dip." Most Western Carolina dips can be characterized as a vinegar/ketchup–based sauce. Dips can be used as a baste mop, a finishing slather, or a post-cooking soak for the meat.

In a large nonreactive bowl, combine all the ingredients and mix well. Make at least 24 hours prior to usage for best flavor. Store the sauce in a tightly covered jar for up to 1 month refrigerated.

BIG BOB'S COMPETITION SWEET SAUCE

MAKES: 2 CUPS

★   ★   ★   ★   ★

1¼ CUPS BIG BOB GIBSON CHAMPIONSHIP RED SAUCE (AVAILABLE AT RETAIL OUTLETS)

⅓ CUP HONEY

¼ CUP BIG BOB GIBSON HABANERO RED SAUCE

2 TABLESPOONS BLACKBERRY JAM

★   ★   ★   ★   ★

In my years of cooking at barbecue competitions, I've noticed that judges' barbecue taste preferences follow trends. In the 1990s, barbecue coated with semisweet tomato-based sauce or even a vinegar sop mop appealed to the average judge. As the years passed the consistent winners on the circuit were using a very sweet tomato-based sauce. These rich glazes started a new trend in competition, whereby most all competitors started sweetening their sauce.

The following recipe is one of my favorite sauces, which I still use in competition as a sweet glaze for pork ribs. This glaze falls in line with the "sweet" trend but still delivers a flavor that doesn't overpower the pork.

Combine the ingredients in a small bowl and blend well. Make at least 24 hours prior to usage for best flavor. Store the sauce in a tightly covered jar for up to 2 weeks in the refrigerator.

HONEY-GARLIC TOMATO SAUCE

MAKES: **2 QUARTS**

COOKING METHOD: **STOVE**

COOKING TIME: **20 MINUTES**

★ ★ ★ ★ ★

2 TABLESPOONS OLIVE OIL

¼ CUP CHOPPED ONION

1 TEASPOON FRESH MINCED GARLIC

4 CUPS KETCHUP

1⅓ CUPS DARK BROWN SUGAR

1 CUP VINEGAR

1 CUP APPLE JUICE

¼ CUP HONEY

1½ TABLESPOONS WORCESTERSHIRE SAUCE

1½ TABLESPOONS LIQUID SMOKE

1 TEASPOON SALT

1 TEASPOON BLACK PEPPER

1 TEASPOON CAYENNE PEPPER

1 TEASPOON CELERY SEED

★ ★ ★ ★ ★

This is an all-purpose barbecue sauce, with a distinct garlic and tomato flavor. We have used this recipe to rave reviews at the James Beard Foundation and the American Institute of Wine and Food's "Best Ribs in America" competition. Use it as a finishing glaze or serve it on the side as a dip for any type of barbecue.

Heat the olive oil in a large nonreactive saucepan over medium heat. Add the onion and garlic and lightly sauté. Stir in the remaining ingredients and heat until the sauce bubbles and starts to steam. Remove from the heat and cool to room temperature. Transfer to a tightly covered jar or plastic container and store refrigerated for up to 2 weeks.

APPLE BOURBON BARBECUE SAUCE

MAKES: 3 CUPS
COOKING METHOD: STOVE
COOKING TIME: 15 MINUTES

★ ★ ★ ★ ★

2 TABLESPOONS BUTTER

¼ CUP DICED SWEET ONION

¾ CUP COARSELY GRATED PEELED APPLE
(PREFERABLY A FIRM, SWEET-FLESHED VARIETY
SUCH AS ROME BEAUTY)

3 TABLESPOONS BOURBON

½ TEASPOON SALT

¼ TEASPOON CAYENNE PEPPER

¼ TEASPOON GROUND CINNAMON

¼ TEASPOON GROUND CUMIN

2 CUPS KETCHUP

½ CUP DISTILLED WHITE VINEGAR

½ CUP COLA

½ CUP BROWN SUGAR

6 TABLESPOONS PURE MAPLE SYRUP

1 TABLESPOON MOLASSES

1 TABLESPOON WORCESTERSHIRE SAUCE

2½ TEASPOONS LIQUID SMOKE

★ ★ ★ ★ ★

This recipe was developed specifically for this book, as a match for the Country-Style Ribs on page 198. Because country-style ribs are bulky and not uniform in appearance, a chunky sauce draws attention to the elements of the sauce and away from the clunky appearance of the ribs themselves. If impressing your guest with fancy plating is not your bag, this sauce is "good eatin'" on just about anything. Besides adding distinct flavor, the bits of apple and sweet onion will add a complementary texture to your barbecue.

In a small skillet, melt the butter over medium heat. Add the onion to the skillet and sauté for 4 minutes. Add the grated apple, bourbon, salt, cayenne pepper, cinnamon, and cumin and sauté for an additional 2 to 3 minutes. Remove from the heat and set aside.

In a large nonreactive saucepan, add the remaining ingredients and mix well. Simmer over medium-low heat for 5 minutes, stirring frequently. Add the apple mixture and stir well. Simmer for 2 additional minutes and remove from the heat. After cooling, transfer to a tightly covered jar or plastic container and store refrigerated for up to 2 weeks.

CAROLINA MUSTARD SAUCE

MAKES: 1¾ CUPS

★ ★ ★ ★ ★

¾ CUP PREPARED YELLOW MUSTARD

½ CUP HONEY

¼ CUP APPLE CIDER VINEGAR

2 TABLESPOONS KETCHUP

1 TABLESPOON BROWN SUGAR

2 TEASPOONS WORCESTERSHIRE SAUCE

1 TEASPOON HOT SAUCE

★ ★ ★ ★ ★

Well, here it is, the bane of North Carolina barbecue. I don't know if it's the addition of mustard that brings frowns to the faces of North Carolina barbecue purists or the fact that this is a South Carolina sauce, but this sauce certainly illustrates the diverging tastes and traditions of barbecue in the Carolinas.

Throughout the 1700s, South Carolina drew a large contingent of immigrant German families. These new settlers brought with them ideas and advancements on ways to farm, as well as an affinity for the flavor of mustard. Even today, many of the families that produce mustard barbecue sauce have a German heritage, most notably the Bessinger family.

In a small bowl, combine all the ingredients and mix well. Make at least 24 hours prior to usage for best flavor. Store refrigerated in a tightly covered jar for up to 2 weeks.

MUSTARD HORSERADISH SAUCE

MAKES: **3 CUPS**

★ ★ ★ ★ ★

1 CUP WHIPPING CREAM

1 CUP MAYONNAISE

¼ CUP PREPARED HORSERADISH

1 TABLESPOON DIJON MUSTARD

1 TEASPOON FRESH LEMON JUICE

⅛ TEASPOON SALT

★ ★ ★ ★ ★

Horseradish is a member of the mustard family, and grating or grinding this edible root releases the volatile oils that produce its signature bite. Mixing the ground horseradish with vinegar tames the spicy heat. German immigrants began growing horseradish in the Mississippi Basin in the late 1800s; today, six million gallons of prepared horseradish are produced there each year, which is 60 percent of the world's supply.

A traditional horseradish sauce is always a great partner with beef and can be as simple as a combination of whipping cream and prepared horseradish. As with any sauce based on whipping cream, the viscosity of the sauce is dependent on how much whipping you do. Here lemon juice and Dijon mustard add a bit of flair to the sauce, while mayonnaise adds a creaminess you can't get from the cream alone.

In a small mixing bowl, beat the whipping cream just until it starts to thicken. Add the remaining ingredients, blend well with a spoon, and serve. Store any leftover sauce in a tightly sealed container and refrigerate for up to 3 days.

CARAMELIZED SOY AND BLACKBERRY GLAZE

MAKES: 1¼ CUPS

COOKING METHOD: STOVE

COOKING TIME: 30 MINUTES

★　★　★　★　★

2 CUPS MIRIN (SWEET RICE WINE)

1¼ CUPS SOY SAUCE

1 CUP SUGAR

½ CUP BLACKBERRY JAM

★　★　★　★　★

On a recent trip to one of my favorite vineyards in California, Seghesio, I stopped by a restaurant in downtown Healdsburg. The sign promising sushi (yes, pitmasters do occasionally enjoy a plate of sushi) drew me to a seat overlooking a fresh seafood bar, where in addition to sushi a wide variety of fried and grilled appetizers was available.

The food was great, but what caught my eye and taste buds was the variety of sauces that accompanied their fresh fare, especially their caramelized soy sauce. This deep black sauce had the consistency of molasses but with a rich chocolate flavor. Surprisingly, it worked very well with the seafood. In my mind I was envisioning chocolate shrimp, chocolate chicken, and chocolate ribs! Well, maybe I got a little carried away, but it did inspire this glaze.

In a small saucepan, combine all the ingredients and mix well. Place over medium-low heat and simmer for 30 minutes, stirring occasionally. The sauce is ready when bubbles rise to the top of the pan. Remove from the heat and set aside until needed. After cooling, transfer to a tightly covered jar or plastic container and store refrigerated for up to 2 weeks. Serve immediately or reheat before serving.

BIG MAMA'S CHILI SAUCE

MAKES: **2 QUARTS**

COOKING METHOD: **STOVE**

COOKING TIME: **45 MINUTES**

★ ★ ★ ★ ★

2 28-OUNCE CANS WHOLE PEELED TOMATOES, DRAINED

4 CUPS DICED ONIONS

3 CUPS SUGAR

1 24-OUNCE JAR APPLESAUCE

2 CUPS DISTILLED WHITE VINEGAR

1 CUP DICED GREEN BELL PEPPER

1 JALAPEÑO PEPPER, SEEDED AND CHOPPED (HOTTER PEPPER CAN BE SUBSTITUTED)

2 TABLESPOONS PICKLING SPICE, TIED IN A CHEESECLOTH POUCH

1½ TABLESPOONS SALT

★ ★ ★ ★ ★

Few culinary terms are as open to interpretation as "chili sauce," and when a recipe calls for chili sauce, there is sometimes a huge lot of confusion about what should be added. Chili sauces can be used as a condiment or an ingredient. They can be hot or mild relative to how much chili pepper goes into the sauce. Chili sauce can be categorized as a hot sauce or a tomato-based condiment similar to ketchup or cocktail sauce. Do you see the confusion?

The best way to describe Big Mama's Chili Sauce is as a cross between a tomato-based condiment and a sweet chow-chow. This chunky sauce has a good mix of sweet and spicy, with the heat determined by the type of pepper used. This particular sauce has always been used as a condiment or topping, but I have found it works well as a finishing sauce for ribs, too. Try it in the morning on scrambled eggs or in a breakfast burrito. Use it instead of relish on hot dogs. Add a dose to beans or peas to heighten their flavor.

Place the tomatoes in a large nonreactive saucepan and use your fingers to mash and separate them into small bits. Add the remaining ingredients and stir well. Bring the sauce to a rolling boil, then reduce the heat and simmer lightly for 45 minutes, or until thickened. Cool the sauce, then chill in an airtight container. Store refrigerated for up to 2 weeks.

PASSION FRUIT BUTTER SAUCE

MAKES: 2 CUPS

COOKING METHOD: STOVE

COOKING TIME: 15 MINUTES

★ ★ ★ ★ ★

2 PASSION FRUITS

3 CUPS WATER

½ CUP SUGAR

8 TABLESPOONS (1 STICK) BUTTER

1 TABLESPOON SALT

★ ★ ★ ★ ★

The passion fruit is native to Brazil, Paraguay, and northern Argentina. It is grown throughout the tropic and near-tropic regions around the world and the pulp, juice, and seeds are used in a variety of ways. The juice is highly concentrated and is used as an additive to other fruit juices. The juice and pulp are used to make pie filling and jellies. The seeds are often used as a topping for salads and other dishes that benefit from an acidic punch.

Passion Fruit Butter Sauce was an inspiration I had when barbecuing in Jamaica. I enjoyed the way the passion fruit was used with seafood there, and I thought it would also complement the flavors of grilled chicken and pork. Use this as a dipping sauce, or better yet as a baste or as a finishing glaze.

Halve the passion fruits, and then scoop out the pulp and seeds. Discard the skin and place the pulp and seeds in a saucepan. Add the water, sugar, and salt and bring to a boil. Reduce the heat, add the butter, and simmer for 10 minutes. Pour the mixture through a strainer and discard the solids. Put the remaining liquid in a tightly sealed jar. Store refrigerated in a tightly sealed container for up to 3 days.

JUST ADD GREENS PEPPER SAUCE

COOKING METHOD: **STOVE**
COOKING TIME: **5 MINUTES**

* * * * *

1 BUNCH OF MIXED PEPPERS (CONTAINER SIZE DETERMINES AMOUNT, DESIRED HOTNESS DICTATES VARIETY)

2 PARTS WHITE BALSAMIC VINAIGRETTE

1 PART APPLE CIDER VINEGAR

* * * * *

In the South, you usually find pepper sauce in the middle of the dinner table beside the salt and black pepper. Don't confuse this pepper sauce with a Tabasco-type sauce; this simple seasoning is made from vinegar and whole peppers. Over time the peppers will flavor the vinegar, and the longer it sits, the better it gets!

Pepper sauce is used as a seasoning and an ornamental decoration. A few dashes will heighten the flavor of black-eyed peas, all types of greens, barbecue, and many other traditional Southern dishes. Pack your pepper sauce in glass containers of any size and shape. The aesthetic value of the glass combined with the color and variety of peppers creates a beautiful conversation piece.

Warm a glass container by submerging it in hot water (this will prevent the glass from cracking when hot vinegar is added). Wash the peppers well and stuff them loosely into the glass container.

Pour both vinegars into a medium-size nonreactive saucepan and cook over medium-high heat. When it reaches a boil, pour the hot vinegar over the peppers, filling the container. Cap the jar and set it aside at room temperature for a few days to allow the vinegar to absorb the pepper flavors. Store the sauce in a tightly covered jar for up to 2 months at room temperature.

CARIBBEAN MOJO SAUCE

MAKES: 3 CUPS

★ ★ ★ ★ ★

20 LIMES

12 GARLIC CLOVES, MINCED

1 CUP EXTRA-VIRGIN OLIVE OIL

½ CUP DRIED OREGANO

1¼ TEASPOONS GROUND CUMIN

★ ★ ★ ★ ★

Mojo is a name that originally branded several varieties of hot sauce from the Canary Islands. Now recipes and uses of mojo are spread throughout the tropical regions of northern South America, Mexico, and the Caribbean. The place of origin of a particular mojo recipe defines both its ingredients and its uses. Ingredients in mojo sauce can include olive oil, garlic, citrus juice (sour orange, lemon, lime), paprika, chili powder, oregano, and cumin. This flavorful sauce can be used on breads, potatoes, salads, and as a seasoning for meats and vegetables.

This recipe was made as a condiment for whole roasted pig. The flavors are a complement to the sour-orange marinade used in Cuban Pig (page 163). The flavor emphasis in this recipe is placed on the acidity of the lime juice, the garlic, and oregano. Mixed with butter, this sauce can be turned into a great topper for sweet potatoes and bread.

Juice the limes into a mixing bowl and add the remaining ingredients. Stir well. Transfer to a tightly sealed jar and store in the refrigerator for up to 4 days.

SOY MARINADE

MAKES: 1½ CUPS

★ ★ ★ ★ ★

1½ CUPS SOY SAUCE

2 TEASPOONS GARLIC POWDER

2 TEASPOONS ONION POWDER

2 TEASPOONS GROUND GINGER

2 TEASPOONS PAPRIKA

2 TEASPOONS SUGAR

2 TEASPOONS MSG (OPTIONAL)

★ ★ ★ ★ ★

For more than fifty years, Alabamians have enjoyed the flavor of steak soaked in a very distinctive soy marinade. In fact, many of the soy-based steak marinades on the market today originated in Alabama. What began as a seasoning for steak has turned into an all-purpose marinade that tastes great on chicken, pork, and vegetables.

Keep in mind when making recipes with soy sauce as an ingredient that your results will vary greatly depending on which brand of sauce you use. Their flavor profiles differ significantly. I like La Choy soy sauce for use in marinades, although I switch to Kikkoman when only a splash is necessary. In recipes like this one, the soy sauce you choose will determine whether your food is edible or disposable!

In a small bowl, combine all the ingredients and mix well. Transfer to a tightly sealed jar and store in the refrigerator for up to 3 weeks.

BARBADO BASTE

MAKES: **1 GALLON**
COOKING METHOD: **STOVE**
COOKING TIME: **5 MINUTES**

★ ★ ★ ★ ★

3 12-OUNCE CANS DARK BEER

3¾ CUPS APPLE CIDER VINEGAR

3¾ CUPS DISTILLED WHITE VINEGAR

3 CUPS (6 STICKS) BUTTER

1½ CUPS WORCESTERSHIRE SAUCE

¾ CUP SOY SAUCE

¼ CUP FRESH LEMON JUICE

9 TABLESPOONS CHILI POWDER

6 TABLESPOONS SALT

3 TABLESPOONS SUGAR

2 TABLESPOONS BLACK PEPPER

2 TABLESPOONS DRY MUSTARD

2 TABLESPOONS PAPRIKA

1 TABLESPOON GROUND CUMIN

★ ★ ★ ★ ★

Barbado is Spanish for goat, but don't be misled by the name; Barbado Baste is an all-purpose baste that is especially good on poultry, pork, beef and, of course, goat.

Barbado Baste works on three fronts: as a flavorizer, moisturizer, and tenderizer. The flavors are intense but give the meat a deep caramelized and slightly tangy taste. Goat meat is especially lean and the liquid baste provides moisture while the butter helps protect the exposed meat from drying out. Vinegar and lemon juice add just enough acid to the mixture to help break down the tough muscles and tenderize the meat.

In a large nonreactive saucepan, combine all the ingredients and mix well. Place over medium-low heat and simmer until the butter melts. Keep the baste on low heat until ready to use. This baste can be made ahead, refrigerated, and reheated before use. Store refrigerated for up to 2 days.

RESOURCES

GOOD READS

Browne, Rick. **The Best Barbecue on Earth.** Berkeley, California, Ten Speed Press, 2008.

Dewitt, Dave, and Nancy Gerlach. **Barbecue Inferno.** Berkeley, California, Ten Speen Press, 2001.

Early, Jim. **The Best Tar Heel Barbecue: Manteo to Murphy.** Winston-Salem, North Carolina, The Best Tar Heel Barbecue, Inc., 2002.

Edge, John T. **Southern Belly.** Athens, Georgia: Hill Street Press, 2000.

Egerton, John. **Cornbread Nation.** Chapel Hill, North Carolina: University of North Carolina Press, 2002.

Elie, Lolis Eric, and Frank Stewart. **Smokestack Lightning: Adventures in the Heart of Barbecue Country.** New York: Farrar, Straus and Giroux, 1996.

Flay, Bobby. **Bobby Flay's Grill It!** New York: Clarkson Potter, 2008.

———. **Bobby Flay's Mesa Grill Cookbook.** New York: Clarkson Potter, 2007.

Garner, Bob. **North Carolina Barbecue: Flavored by Time.** Winston-Salem, North Carolina: John F. Blair, 1996.

Jamison, Cheryl and Bill. **Smoke & Spice.** Boston, Massachusetts: Harvard Common Press, 2004.

Kirk, Paul. **Paul Kirk's Championship Barbecue.** Boston, Massachusetts: Harvard Common Press, 2004.

———. **Paul Kirk's Championship Barbecue Sauces.** Boston, Massachusetts: Harvard Common Press, 1998.

Lampe, Ray. **Dr. BBQ's Big-Time Barbecue Cookbook.** New York: St. Martin's Griffin, 2005.

———. **Dr. BBQ's Barbecue Road Trip.** New York: St. Martin's Griffin, 2007.

Mills, Mike, and Amy Mills Tunnicliffe. **Peace Love and Barbecue.** New York: Rodale, 2005.

Raichlen, Steven. **The Barbecue Bible.** New York: Workman, 1998.

———. **How to Grill.** New York: Workman, 2001.

Walsh, Rob. **Legends of Texas Barbecue Cookbook: Recipes and Recollections from the Pit Bosses.** San Francisco, California: Chronicle, 2002.

PUBLICATIONS

Fiery Foods & BBQ
3825 Beall Court SW
Albuquerque, New Mexico 87105
505-873-8680
fiery-foods.com

Kansas City BullSheet
11514 Hickman Mills Drive
Kansas City, Missouri 64134
1-800-963-5227
kcbs.us

National Barbecue News
215 Peterson Ave.
Douglas, Georgia 31534-0981
1-800-385-0002
barbecuenews.com

★ ★ ★ ★ ★

ORGANIZATIONS

International Barbeque
Cookers Association (IBCA)
P.O. Box 200556
Arlington, Texas 76007
817-469-1579
ibcabbq.org

Kansas City Barbeque Society
11514 Hickman Mills Drive
Kansas City, Missouri 64134
816-765-5891
kcbs.us

National Barbecue Association
8317 Cross Park Drive,
Suite 150
P.O. Box 140647
Austin, Texas 78714-0647
888-909-2121

Memphis Barbecue Network
6972 Appling Farms Parkway
Suite 106
Memphis, Tennessee 38133
mbnbbq.com

Southern Foodways Alliance
Center for the Study of
Southern Culture
Barnard Observatory
University, Mississippi 38677
662-915-5993
southernfoodways.com

There are several state and regional
barbecue organizations, including: Florida
Barbecue Association, California Barbecue
Association, Arizona BBQ Association, South
Carolina Barbeque Association, Central
Texas Barbecue Association, Pacific North-
west BBQ Asssociation, New England
Barbecue Society, Alabama Barbecue
Association, Mid Atlantic BBQ Association,
Rocky Mountain BBQ Association and others.

CUSTOM COOKERS, SMOKERS, AND GRILLS

American Barbecue Systems
15612 South Keeler Terrace
Olathe, Kansas 66062
913-254-1600
americanbarbecuesystems.com

Backwoods Smoker
8245 Dixie Shreveport Rd.
Shreveport, Louisiana 71107
318-220-0380
backwoods-smoker.com

BBQ Pits by Klose
2216 West 34th Street
Houston, Texas 77018
713-686-8720
bbqpits.com

Big Green Egg
3417 Lawrenceville Highway
Tucker, Georgia 30084
770-938-9394
biggreenegg.com

Cookshack
2304 N. Ash St.
Ponca, Oklahoma 74601
800-423-0698
cookshack.com

Horizon Smoker Company
802 North 15th
Perry, Oklahoma 73077
580-336-2800
horizonbbqsmokers.com

Jacks Old South Cookers
2732 Pine St.
Unadilla, Georgia 31091
jacksoldsouth.com

Jambo Pits
P.O. Box 40326
Fort Worth, Texas 76140-0326

817-223-3918
jambopits.com

JedMaster
22251 Diesel Drive
McCalla, Alabama 35111
866-568-8200
brittsbarbecue.com

Kingfisher Kookers
201 North 13th St
Kingfisher, Oklahoma 73750
866-542-5665
kingfisherkookers.com

**Komodo Kamado
Refractory Cookers**
Surabaya, Indonesia
310-928-3648 Los Angeles
404-418-6648 Atlanta
komodokamado.com

Lang BBQ Grills
U.S. Highway 82 West
Nahunta, Georgia 31553
800-462-4629
pigroast.com

Ole Hickory Pits
333 North Main Street
Cape Girardeau, Missouri 63701
800-223-9667
olehickorypits.com

Peoria Custom Cookers
5103 N. University St.
Peoria, Illinois 61014
866-404-4745
peoriacustomcookers.com

Southern Pride
5003 Meadowland Parkway
Marion, Illinois 62959
800-851-8180
southernpride.com

Spicewine Ironworks
1333 Business Loop 70 East
Columbia, Missouri 65201
573-881-4042
spicewineironworks.com

Stump's Smokers
103-C Industrial Way
Centerville, Georgia 31028
866-609-6455
stumpssmokers.com

Tucker Cookers
122 West Carolina Ave
Memphis, Tennessee 38103-4612
901-578-3221
tuckercooker.com

Weber
200 East Daniels Road
Palatine, Illinois 60067
800-446-1071
weberbbq.com

MEAT PURVEYORS
Allen Brothers
3737 South Halsted Street
Chicago, Illinois 60609
800-957-0111
allenbrothers.com

Brandt Beef
P.O. Box 118
Brawley, California 92227
brandtbeef.com

Jamison Farm
171 Jamison Lane
Latrobe, Pennsylvania 15650
800-237-5262
jamisonfarm.com

Montana Legend
115 South Broadway, Suite 1
P.O. Box 209
Red Lodge, Montana 59068

800-838-5657
montanalegend.com

Snake River Farms
1555 Shoreline Drive, 3rd floor
Boise, Idaho 83702
208-250-0067
snakeriverfarms.com

SPICES
Pendery's
1221 Manufacturing Street
Dallas, Texas 75207
800-533-1870
penderys.com

The Spice House
1031 North Old World
Third Street
Milwaukee, Wisconsin 53203
414-272-0977
www.thespicehouse.com

Vanns Spices Ltd.
1716 Whitehead Rd
Suite A
Baltimore, Maryland 21207
410-944-3888
vannsspices.com

WOOD
Peoples Woods
75 Mill Street
Cumberland, Rhode Island
02864
800-729-5800
peopleswoods.com

SmokinLicious
110 North 2nd Street
Olean, New York 14760
800-941-5054
smokinlicious.com

W W Wood Inc.
1799 Corgey Road
Pleasanton, Texas 78064
830-569-2501
woodinc.com

SUPPLIES & ACCESSORIES
Hawgeyes BBQ
1313 S.W. Ordnance Rd
Ankeny, Iowa 50021
877-841-7192
hawgeyesbbq.com

**Tel-Tru Manufacturing
(thermometers)**
408 St. Paul Street
Rochester, New York 14605
800-232-5335
teltru.com

The BBQ GURU
357 Ivyland Road
Warminster, Pennsylvania 18974
800-288-4878
thebbqguru.com

The Kansas City BBQ Store
11946 Strang Line Rd
Olathe, Kansas 66062
913-782-5171
thekansascitybbqstore.com

BIG BOB GIBSON BAR-B-Q
bigbobgibson.com
1715 6th Ave SE
Decatur, Alabama 35601
877-350-0404
256-350-6969

2520 Danville Rd SW
Decatur, Alabama
256-350-0404

1507 W Roosevelt Rd
Monroe, North Carolina 28110
704-289-5102

ACKNOWLEDGMENTS

Saying you are writing a book is the easy part; actually doing it is a full-time commitment. From the first day when I sat staring at my computer screen wondering how to begin and thinking, "What have I got myself into?" this book has been like a difficult child who some days I have enjoyed and others have made me want to scream. But looking back at this completed manuscript, I have nothing but feelings of fulfillment—not from what I have accomplished but from the effort of many others who have tirelessly labored hard on my behalf. If you ever think your friends are few, write a book and appreciate all of the love and support you often take for granted.

My first thanks go to my wife, Amy, who has not only understood my long hours strapped to the computer and endless hours hovering over the backyard grill, but has been supportive during my barbecue sabbatical. I could always trust her to give me an honest opinion on the recipes I experimented with, or work through the recipes herself. She made this book better!

Anyone who has ever met Don and Carolyn McLemore knows I can say "in-laws" with pride. They provide an atmosphere of love and support and share this wonderful barbecue experience with me every day. Without their hard work running the restaurants when I had to meet a deadline, this book would not have been possible.

I have had many wonderful experiences writing this book, but none were more pleasurable than the time spent with Big Bob's youngest child, Ruth Hopkins. I will cherish the afternoons we spent while she reminisced about old times, the family, and the restaurants.

I couldn't have done this without the unfailing support and guidance of Clarkson Potter Publishers. Special thanks go to Pam Krauss for giving me the opportunity to work with so many talented people and for walking me through the first stage of writing a book. To one of my newest best friends, senior editor Judy Pray, who got stuck with a rookie writer but patiently and professionally held my hand. Thanks to senior editor Rica Allannic for tending the fire in the last hour of cooking. This book benefited from her knowledge and expert touch. Marketing director Donna Passannante and publicity director Kate Tyler took to this project with a zeal as if it were their own book. I am indebted to them. Publisher Lauren Shakely, whose time and productive effort helped make this barbecue book a reality. When I pick up this book and smile, I think of art director Jane Treuhaft, who, with design from Subtitle, transformed chaos into something so visually appealing. I could never forget about Ashley Phillips and Peggy Paul, who worked behind the scenes organizing and assisting with this book

★ ★ ★ ★ ★

but most of all could brighten my day with a phone call. An enormous amount of my respect goes to Doris Cooper for putting together the best team in all of publishing! Thank you all for believing in me and this book project.

Carrie Bachmann is a publicist extraordinaire. When she is involved, as they say in the South, "Grab it and hang on!"

There is a group of people who shared with me one of the most demanding and intense weeks of my life, the photo shoot. My photographer, Ben Fink, flawlessly captured the essence of barbecue through his storytelling photos. I was lucky to have Pam Lolley to add her expert touch to my barbecue with both food styling and prop selection. Carolyn McLemore, Amy Lilly, Sandra Cordonis, and Sarah Mattox took a huge weight from my shoulders by gathering and cooking some of the family favorite recipes contained in these pages. Big thanks also go to Ginger Bramlett, who is a hardworking photo assistant and a great friend.

My literary agent, Angela Miller, opened my eyes to a new world and was always there to make sure I didn't misstep as I trudged through the new experience of writing a book.

When your day is filled with throwing more logs on the fire, you question whether you can actually write a book. It helps to have people you trust to answer that question for you. Thanks to my sister, Tina, for being there and giving me confidence. Thank you, John Markus for your support and providing me a batter board for ideas.

Huge thanks to all of the pitmasters and barbecue fanatics whom I can truly call friends; who have never been bashful about giving away advice and secrets. I can't mention one without mentioning all, and I can't mention everyone without writing another chapter. This book is filled with the knowledge we have shared for more than a decade during our all-night cooks.

Companies within the barbecue industry are filled with the most generous and hospitable people I know, none more than Kingsford charcoal. Thank you for your contribution to barbecue and your valued friendships.

Finally, a debt of gratitude goes to the entire staff of Big Bob Gibson Bar-B-Q. Their hard work and dedication provided me the extra time I needed to write a book. I couldn't ask for a better team. Their confidence and pride are unwavering.

In the early 1920s, Big Bob Gibson's backyard barbecues were times to celebrate life with family and friends.

INDEX

Page numbers in **bold** refer to photographs.

★ ★ ★ ★ ★